TIME MANIPULATION:

THE 24/8 MINDSET

24 hours a day, 8-day work week…

By Chanclor Burnett

Copyright © 2021 Chanclor Burnett

All rights reserved. No part of this book may be reproduced or used in any manner without the prior written permission of the copyright owner, except for the use of brief quotations in a book review.

I have changed some names to protect individuals' privacy. To maintain the anonymity of the individuals involved, I have changed some details. The information in this book was correct at the time of publication, but the Author does not assume any liability for loss or damage caused by errors or omissions. These are my memories, from my perspective, and I have tried to represent events as faithfully as possible.

Contact Information: Happyhomesllc74@gmail.com

I like to give credit to the people who have earned it:

Edited by Javaid Nasir (Fiverr)
Cover art by Priticreative (Fiverr)

Introduction

This is a book that means a great amount to me for its service that I hope I it'll give to the world. This is not a book intending to grant me self-gratification or awareness. this book is a manual of advice that I have experienced, these are methods that self hardly experienced or experienced through another. There are methods that serve an overall purpose in order to make you successful in your own right.

This book is not an attempt to force feed my thoughts and ways upon the reader. I am not commissioning on my way or the highway philosophy. Nor an attempt to say that my methods are the only true way to success because that's ridiculous to even imply. Please don't assume that I am a model citizen of the upmost education, as I am not. I am no saint, although I am working to better this fact.

I am a convicted felon from Jackson Mississippi and a proud brother of block ethnicity. I am from a middle-class household and raised by a proud black mother. I earned my GED from Job corps in Crystal Springs MS in which I used to graduate college. I am a proud owner of multiple businesses from different trades. Each business has employed people of need and have been successful in their own right. I still must declare to you that this book is not for me.

This book is for the young adults who don't have guidance. This is for our young brothers and sisters who are missing a parental figure, or who lacks sufficient role models. Growing up most of us idolized the rappers, actors, as well as the entrepreneurs of our time. Which tends to lead us into the study of pimping, prostitution, thievery and so on. The dope boys are the visible successful business owners. The strippers and whores seem to be the only women who can afford to wear the latest in fashion. This book is meant to emphasize the bigger picture.

This book is written for the prisoners who are behind the walls and fences who don't have an idea of where to start. Remember that a felony is not a financial death sentence. This is not an end to a means but the beginning of a new road, I know that you've heard it all from "minor setbacks for a major comeback" to "ball and chill". This is not an attempt at another quotable cliché or a one-line gimmick. This is a guidebook to help you reintegrate.

This book is also for the uneducated because you don't need a college degree to understand these methods. Please don't assume this book is only targeting a specify audience or race. This is not just for blacks or felons. This book is intended to inform with universal appeal and knowledge so don't assume and make an ass out of yourself.

I write this book for the reader who understands that time equals money. That we are granted the same 24 hours in a day but it's how you choose to use yours that makes you successful, the book of Ecclesiastes tells us that "life is but a wind". we should enjoy our life to the fullest and strive to be the best that we can. This book is meant to spark ambition and instill productivity in your life by any means should you take for granted and allow it to waste away.

I remember when I was 18 and overdosed on ecstasy, I fell face first into the concrete driveway at my mother's house. I immediately hopped to my feet and ran to the front room couch. As I sat there my entire life passed before my eyes. When I came to reality and calmed myself down, I had realized the cold truth of the matter. The truth is that besides, my beautiful son and daughter, I had not accomplished anything worthy in my life. I had no legacy to leave behind and no wealth to help my next generation of offspring. With that being said, I want you to sit the book down and think to yourself "what have I accomplished to leave behind?" Now ask yourself; "is it enough?" now let's move on and I welcome you to a world of 24 hours and 8 day work weeks.

Section 1: The Basics

Chapter 1: Presentation

The year was 2015 and I was attending Hinds community college in Jackson, MS. This was a great year indeed for this year I was firing on all cylinders. I had just begun to operate my businesses in a profitable matter, and I was drawing a lot of my clientele through my advertisement methods. I was engaged to be married to a beautiful young woman and we were in the process of buying a home for us and our two-year-old daughter. This was also the year I was set to graduate from college with a associates degree in computer science technology. I had a lot going on at 27 years old and I was happy with my busy schedule.

I usually began my days in a flurry of quick movements in which I always turn back to make sure I wasn't omitting some chare. I always have been an early riser because where I come from the earlier you wake the more money you make. I'll be in the restroom brushing my teeth and washing my face with a sense of urgency. I wore my hair in a spikey fro which was lined up with a fresh taper cut. I would rub some petroleum jelly over my face and continue to work some through my thick and curly black hair in order to get my style just right. That style was a mixture of nonexistent and I don't give a care. If the females love it, I loved it, I felt great.

Then I would head to my room to get dressed in my outfit that I picked out for that day. My day-to-day attire normally consisted of some sweater with my favorite artists on it such as Tupac, Aaliyah, Big Pun, Left Eye and so on. My pants were always either Evisu jeans, crown holder or Levi's. I would complete this ensemble with my favorite brand tennis shoes at the time, which were usually 95' Air Max. I would spray some of the best smelling cologne that I could afford to make sure I smelled immaculate when I'm in close range. Then run out the door grabbing my keys, and wallet while placing my diamond stuff earing in my left earlobe.

I'll get into my 2007 Mercury Montego which contained all black leather interior. I truly loved the car because even though it was eight years old it drew the attention that I wanted. Ill crank up that radio blasting the hottest trap music of that time then fire up a Newport cigarette. As I head for school, I would notice the people that were out and about commuting would watch as I pass by with fascination, I would look straight with occasionally catching a glimpse at them as I was rapping the song word for word.

When I finally got to campus, I would walk the halls with a mixture of swagger and purpose. My fellow students could see the look of confidence and determination in my face. I'll be greeted by several people from students to staff because I was known mostly through networking. I would post flyers, pass out business cards and more. It didn't hurt that I was one of the top student technicians there on campus, and I would fix a good portion of student devices on campus. I was truly on my way to success but there was more I needed to learn.

My professor was Mr. Adell Brooks. He was an older black man who acquired a good amount of money as a computer technician in the earlier stages, a very charismatic and professional man who also was a mentor to me. He would challenge each of his students with tasks that took a good amount of skill but will give us a great amount of knowledge. I loved his class and excelled within his program.

So, one day after class was over, I stayed back in the lab as I would usually do to fix some clients computers. There were normally a few other students there as well who were still working on their projects and the other on site student technician. We started talking as we usually do joking around and talking about techie subjects. Then Mr. Brooks asked a serious question that changed my outlook on day-to-day presentation.

Mr. Brooks asked me, "Who do you think is my best student?" It became a bit quiet as the group anticipated my answer. "Me," I replied as he followed with a quick question "Why is that?" To me my answer was reasonable and had been obvious to me over the past year and a half. Our class consisted of mostly geeks who although they were of good intelligence, they lacked people skills. I was more of a complete subject because not only were I a geek but also very charismatic around people. I had long concluded that I was the best student in the program.

After expressing this fact, the group then turned to Mr. Brooks awaiting his response. He didn't flinch and responding, "Chanclor that is true. You are my best student but there is much you need to change in order to be successful. It maybe as a result of your previous background that you are from, but you present yourself as more of a hood than a technician." He then made a statement that caused me to think, "With your appearance and delivery it seems more like you are attempting to conduct an illegal transaction rather than completing a technical order."

In all honesty Mr. Brooks was totally correct in his statement. I grew up in Jackson, Mississippi and my family was from a neighborhood called "Shady Oaks". Although I came from a great household with a wonderful mother, I couldn't help but to be in the streets. From the age of 14 I began selling marijuana to other students in middle school and adults at home. I considered myself a hustler because I would also sell single cigarettes, bootleg CDs and DVDs, candy and snacks. So, you can say I had a knack for business at a young age.

As I became older, I began to be more observant of my surroundings. Even though I was very intelligent and had a gift with servicing and repairing computers I was infatuated with the street life. My favorite rapper was Tupac Shakur, and I grew up idolizing the dope boys and pimps in my neighborhood. I wanted to live their lives and encompass their bravado. All this combined with my motivation to make money affected my appearance. So, when I finally got home, I looked up my Facebook to check out my pictures. That's when I realized that I indeed dressed and come across as a dope boy.

This realization opened my eyes to my true presentation, and I began to understand that in order to be the part I had to dress the part. I took inventory of the technicians that I came in to contact with and although their overall attire differed from one another, their clothing expressed the same point. Their appearance oozed of professionalism and techy. When you looked at them you were almost certain your technical issues will be solved. I knew then that it was time for a change.

So over time I began to dress more technical casual. Most of my shirts became Polo shirts of a more fitted sizing. My Levi jeans were crisper and were adjusted with a belt in order to stay upon my waist. Of course, I still wore sneakers from time to time but now I began to wear more casual shoes and boots. This change really boosted my business, and this made Mr. Brooks more confident in his best students.

Conclusion:

This is an important point to be made for any person trying to kick down the door opportunity. Whether you're a young person attempting to impress a superior in order to work your way up past your position. You may be a recently released brother or sister who needs to just dress the part in order to get hired for a new job. The bible states that you can tell the kind of tree by the fruit that it produces.

The truth of the matter is that you don't have to spend an abundance of money on your wardrobe to provide yourself with presentable threads. For instance, two of the world wealthiest men, Warren Buffet and Bill Gates, are hardly ever caught in public wearing designer. These clothes don't have to be the costliest of brands that will hurt your pockets. There are many affordable brands that you can find in department stores in your local indoor or outdoor malls.

If you do prefer the more popular brands such as Polo, Izod, Nautica, etc. then these clothes are still available in your price range. Take the time and browse some secondhand thrift stores in your area. These stores make their money by dealing in used but good quality clothes and other items for a low price. You will be able to find some of your favorite brands on occasion, but the correct size can be rather difficult to find. For my audience that have recently been released from prison, these stores are great places to shop. Most of the thrift stores donate clothes and other items to people who are fresh out.

Shopping online is the way of the world and will be for a very long time. You can find a great number of deals for clothes that are on sale. All it takes is a quick google search to render countless number of websites that are eager to please. There are many discount apps that you can download through your mobile device's iTunes or google play store. Facebook also has a great feature that allows user to sell used or new items online. Most cities have secured meet up areas strictly for these transactions.

For our newly or soon to be released readers there are many opportunities that are available to you. There are non-profit organizations that grant clothing vouchers and work clothes.. These same places offer help with purchasing hygiene products as well. Although we don't like them, most probation offices are allotted a second chance budget dedicated just for these causes. Don't ever be too proud that you don't use the resources granted to you because closed mouths don't get fed.

Remember to always make sure that you are presentable before you make an appearance. This goes for social media as well. You never know who will see you when you are out. The person who will be conducting your interview for your next job position could be your friend on Facebook, and just saw your latest posts. Besides, you can always dress however you want on your personal time. When I am just having a beer with the guys, I am back in my

Nike sweats and Air Max. It's not always what you do but how you do it.

CHAPTER 2:

Employment:

Now that we are dressed in the proper attire and ready to present ourselves, let's find us a decent job. Whether your goals include owning and/or managing your own business, investing, or real estate; a regular 9 to 5 is usually the best start. When you are beginning your journey to success, a job is more than just for sure check but it's like your backbone. This gig isn't meant to make you rich but to be a steppingstone to pay for necessities and bills. Depending on your plans this job can be just something to get you by or if you get lucky it can be a career or a trade,

So, whether you're a youngster looking for one of your first gigs or an adult looking for your next, the best way to begin is by building a suitable resume'. A resume' is a representation of you and your prior experience. The key is to dress it up as presentable as possible in order to persuade the employer. Its best to keep a thesaurus on hand in order to be able to use a more extensive vocabulary. You want to be sure that you are using a professional font, font size, color and type face. This is a resume' not a club opening flyer.

This resume' will be your introduction to the employer even before you meet them in person. Be sure to include some of your best work and sociable qualities. It's good to list such qualities as "hard working, ambitious, trustworthy, charismatic, etc." because employers look for these in potential candidates. Remember to tailor your resume' to the employer that you apply for because some qualities are better adjusted for certain employers.

You'll want to list any prior experiences that you've had. This gives the employer an glimpse of your work history and helps to profile your tendencies. I must caution to my readers that are new to the workforce, do not fret. Take this time now to list any volunteer work, side jobs, etc. that you've had experience with. Recently released readers, remember to list as much as you can that is relatable to the job. You want to fill in as much gapped time of absence by listing any jobs that you held down in the facility, The worst thing to do is to leave an unexplained gap in your career. The best thing to do is have a strategy to explain your situation ahead of time. Most employers will conduct a background check anyway so it's best to jump in front and confront the situation head on.

Education is a very important field as well for the employers that are looking over your application. They want to use this information in order to learn the tasks and positions that you qualify for. A G.E.D. or high school diploma are usually enough to get you hired at most entry level jobs. If you happen to have college degrees and/or certifications this will be the best time to let them know. As you can probably already realize that these accomplishments can make a candidate much more desirable. If you don't have much of an history just list any marketable skills that you have accomplished. Do not let any lack of progress in any of these fields get you down because there always somebody willing to hire you.

I know that you've heard it countless times that it's not what you know but who you know. This is so true so please be considerate of who you interact with on a day-to-day basis because they could become a reference. You want to be able to list any businesses/work aquaintance that you've been able to establish a relationship over the years. Even if you are lacking in this department, you may list some references that can vouch for your character such as, professors, counselors, etc. This section is important as well because employers follow up upon these ,so a decent report can take you long way.

If you are having trouble with creating your resume' here are multiple ways to get you started. Most of the word processors that can be installed on your device comes with templates of resumes. You can use these templates to edit them and insert your own information. Templates are editable examples of a form that you are able to personalize to your specific information. Some employment websites offer built in resume building tools such as Indeed, Zip recruiter, etc.

After you've finally completed the masterpiece that is your resume' it is time to apply for a job. Keep in mind that unless you are looking for a specific career, that job applications are basically a numbers game.

Think of it in terms of statistics; for every 15 applications you will receive 7 follow up calls. Surely out of those 7 follow up calls at least 2 are potential hires. Be conscious of popular opinion that in most cases any decent jobs beat no job because we all need positive cash flow. Please don't misunderstand, never turn down a job unless it's a job that is demeaning to you or a job that you don't want because you want to be able to stay mentally sufficient. Although, I'm not saying to be too picky but remember this, is not the end of your journey. Just be sure to make a good show of work ethic, character, and be sure to give two weeks' notice if and whenever you're ready to move on. These actions will make for a good reference when you apply for a better employment opportunity.

Now a days a great number of employers use the internet to find potential job candidates. There are countless websites that you can find through a google search. Sometimes it is best to apply through the business's official business website because this will eliminate third party representatives. These websites usually offer an option for you to upload your resume' to help you speed through the application process. So, keep you a copy of your resume' on your devices and/or on a portable junk drive.

Most of all, you must know that some of these online applications require an assessment to be completed before you can submit your application. These assessments usually ask a series of questions that you'll answer on a scaling system that give options such as "least likely and most likely". Some of these tests are more of problem-solving exercises that relate to the position that you are applying for. These assessments are meant to study you from a mental aspect to decide your mental capacity to handle the position. Be sure to answer these questions in relativity with the position that you are applying for and ne quick because most are timed.

There are job search apps that you can download directly to your mobile device at your app store. I personally have used Indeed,this site and websites similar are popular and are simple to use. These apps are usually the quickest because you can upload your resume' directly through the app. Once the upload is completed, initiate a search of available jobs by the type of jobs you are applying for. After an efficient search has been performed, then submit you application, and this process will be complete. The wonderful thing is that this one click submission allow for you to apply to a great number of applications in a small amount of time. Also, after your've completed an assessment you have the choice of using your previous results next time so that you don't have to be tedious. Remember it's only a numbers game.

Sometimes cold calls and walk ins are successful as well. If you are still having trouble after using these suggestions, then it's time to take a more direct route. Sit down and simply go through your local phonebook and call businesses to ask if they are hiring because this can help. Even just going in and asking a manager if they're hiring can seriously aid the hiring process. These strategies can be quite fruitful because some companies haven't taken on the online process yet. These businesses usually still incorporate the use of paper applications. And hire help through advertising on signs and/or word of mouth.

Social media isn't just for posting pictures of your new car, updating your friend list, or to edit your on and off again relationship status. These platforms are great for being used as a networking tool. Facebook offers employment groups in order to share businesses that are currently hiring. A lot of these places offer applications directly through Facebook to make the process easier. Some social media platforms such as LinkedIn, are mainly career based platforms. LinkedIn allows users to upload their resumes and network with other professionals. This helps the users to find jobs instantly. If all this fails, then just update your status to "Need a job."

Finally, take advantage of the hiring professionals. Every state has a job center that offers tons of resources to get a job. A lot of companies enlist their positions through these centers to acquire quality employees. Try a staffing agency as well. These agencies have contracts with companies in order to get them good workers on call. A lot of these jobs are short term, but they can become long-term depending on the quality of your work. Although, most staffing agencies have contracts that won't allow for their clients to hire you on directly to their company for a certain time period. These agencies are being paid for their services and they take their service fees off the top of your pay.

When you receive the call that its time for an interview its time to put that new appearance to work. Make sure to show up to the interview a proper attire no matter how low down the chain of power that the position is. Remember first impressions are everything. When preparing for the interview, take the time to look up the business to see what kind of skills and qualities that they expect from their employees. Be ready to integrate them in conversation at will. If the position needs a great amount of speed, then be ready to speak of times that you've used your speed.

When at the interview always pay attention to your surroundings because most of the time this offers clues to what you can add to the conversation. Once you are sitting across from your interviewer be sure to pour on the charm. Give a firm handshake and try to keep a sociable amount of eye contact. It always helps to smile from time to time to give respect to the interviewer's position and show interest. Try not to stutter or fumble your words up because this can be a negative sign and can show nervousness. Overall, just be your great self and secure the bag.

Conclusion:

A job is a very important part of your success plan, so be persistant in your job search. This job will help lay the foundation for everything that you are planning to accomplish. Remember, if you don't work, you don't eat and if you don't grind then you don't shine. It's not a bad idea to have two jobs at first in order to have more money to save. It is best to generate as much cash flow as possible because bills and life gets expensive. Sometimes finding that first job can really be tough but never let up.

For the young readers, be sure to apply for jobs that tailor to your age range. Places like grocery stores, fast food restaurants, department stores, etc. are usually quick to hire young employees. Most of these jobs are great for students because they are usually willing to work with a school schedule. Sometimes, labor jobs are quick to grant summer jobs to younger employees for their strength and will to learn. Just remember that for the most part that if you have bigger ambitions then be sure to keep in mind that these jobs aren't forever.

Most felons and freshly released job seekers face rough hiring opportunities. Some states don't allow the felony question on the application process but some still do. Even if they dont ask the question, then a background check will give them the information. If you see the question you must check yes of course but that doesn't eliminate you from the job. Some applications ask if you've been convicted of a felony in the last 7 years which helps for those of you with old felonies. There are companies that don't mind felonies at all and these are called felony friendly. Check the resources sections for a list. Most labor jobs require hard work but they are felony friendly. So remember that where there is a will there is a way.

Last but not least, to all my readers who are up there a bit in age that are attempting to get back in the work force, there are plenty of jobs that look to hire seasoned vets. The way that society is today, the workforce lacks a lot of the qualities that come naturally in the older generation. Where you seem to lack in youth and virile, you will be strong in character and ethics. Don't get yourself down in the dumps behind age but be proud of your wisdom.

CHAPTER 3

Bank Accounts:

Bank accounts are as pivotal to your success as your job is. If you are going to be earning, saving and spending money then a bank account is the next reasonable option after starting a new job. The world is drifting farther and farther away from using physical cash and banks offer accounts that help you to carry less cash on you. Even from a safety point of view, less physical cash the better. There are other options to eliminate the day to day use of cash such as; prepaid debit cards but a bank account is always the best choice.

There are two types of account that banks offer; checking and saving account. I suggest that when opening a account with a bank opt for both accounts because each one offers different features. Saving accounts are great for holding money for a longer period of time because unlike a checking account, a savings account earns interest. You can receive an ATM card by only using this account but with this card you can't swipe at stores, order online, send money, etc. This card is strictly for ATM purposes.

A checking account is more advanced, and morewidely used. These accounts are usually backed by the savings account but most do not offer the feature of drawing interest. Checking accounts are designed for purchasing items and paying bills; so you only store money that you plan to spend on this account. These accounts offer a card that is usually powered by Visa, Mastercard, etc. and they are available to spend everywhere, even online. This is the main account that you need when starting off.

Checking accounts offer a great number of features but one of the more important features is overdraft protection. Overdraft protection is a small loan from the bank to the account holder which is meant to build a relationship between the two of you. Overdraft protection functions as a safety net for when you swipe your card and funds aren't available at the time of purchase. The bank then loans you the money to complete your transaction without the embarrassment of being declinesd This loan comes with a fee for each overdraft purchase which is usually between $30.00 to $50.00. The bank only allows a certain amount of overdraft protection per account, but as you gain a relationship the amount grows.

Overdraft protection is a great tool for building a great relationship with an bank. It is also the most abused features on a bank account. A lot of immature and naïve account holders max out their overdraft protection and leave the negative status outstanding. This is a short-lived solution to any problem that can come back to bite you. A lot of banks mark this as a negative mark on your credit score and this makes it harder to open another bank account in the future. Don't allow a small moment of misjudgment to destroy a possibly good financial partnership.

There are many different kinds of banks as well that specialize in different areas. The main two that I use are banks and credit unions. A good bank is usually a bank that is worldwide, so that you may find one almost anywhere you travel. The banks usually deal with more money and therefore are easier to get loans from for certain businesses. Credit unions are usually community based, which means that they mostly only operate in that state or region. Although, most credit unions have sister/brother banks in other states to help with this. Credit unions deal with less money than a worldwide bank and are usually keen to helping account holders that plan to operate in the local community. Therefore, as you build a relationship with each other over time you can do great business. Take the time to conduct further research of the differences of these two institutions so that you make a good choice.

To start an account with a bank you must have a few things that we will discuss here. First, you will need at least two forms of identification but the main id should be a picture id. The second form of identification can either be a birth certificate or a social security card. You may or may not need a proof of address of some sorts such as utility bill, lease agreement, mail etc. Most banks require an initial deposit to start an account with them. this amount may very but is usually between $1.00 to$100.00. After opening the account and activating your card, these funds are assessable immediately. There are some bank fees for some banks and you should be careful to read what fees your account will be charged. Most fees can be waved with the use of direct deposit.

Its payday and you've collected your check but you have to make it to the bank before 6:00 pm. You may have a busy day ahead of you, so you wish you could skip some of these steps. Instead of heading to the bank waiting in line to deposit or cash your check, just use direct deposit. Most jobs offer direct deposit to be more expedient, efficient and eliminate the process of paper checking. While using this option you will gain an assortment of benefits.

Direct deposit is a means to strengthen your relationship with your bank. Banks tend to monitor account's active cash flow, which is based on how much is deposited, and spent. As a bank begins note the positive flow of money that is constantly being deposited, like a pay check every one or two weeks, they begin to trust the account more. This allows the bank to waive some fees that they usually charge for maintenance. The longer you keep an account open with this positive cash flow the more loan options that become available to you. A bank will approve you for a bigger overdraft protection and if you will apply for a loan one day then this will help you.

As you begin to make more money, be sure to save some

of this income. Any money that you're not planning on spending in the near future, deposit in the saving saccount. This will allow your money to draw a small amount of interest while in turn waiving your maintenance fee and keeping your account active. Try to keep a goal for savings in order to keep you motivated while trying to reach your goals. This savings will come in handy when you are ready to invest.

Most of you want to save to prepare yourself for rainy days or tribulations. There are unexpected costs at every turn and you never know when a new bill will pop up. Try to save at least three months' worth of bills and rent. This will help you with the random costs, but most of all this will give you a cushion when you're ready to jump into business and investing. Don't ever assume anything and never live day to day if you can help it. Saving takes some self-discipline but don't get caught up in trying to save everything in the beginning, because you must spend money to make money in one form or another.

Conclusion

Growing up in my neighborhood around my peers a bank wasn't the norm. Most people that I knew grew up not being able to trust banks because of something they heard from someone else , they experienced once before, or their just post plain paranoid. The people that I saw making tons of money were "dope boys" and "pimps" and these entrepreneurs didn't frequent banks at all. A lot of teenagers grow up like this and they tend to distrust the banking system. This is why I am grateful for growing up in my household.

My mother worked as a registered nurse for the local hospital, and she was enlisted in the Army reserves. My mother earned a college degree, multiple certifications, military accomplishments and she was great with money. She instilled a lot of her valves within me. I received a weekly allowance for the chores I completed. Instead of cash my mother opened a bank account for me to teach me the importance of having an account. She would then pay me through my bank account while teaching me about savings. This gave me a nice head start in the knowledge department of banking.

This is a practice that I recommend to the parents of this generation. When your children reaches the age of 12 to 14 years old, it is a wonderful idea to begin teaching them about finances. This is an important part of life that should be taught right along with school subject s such as english, mathematics, history, etc. Most schools fail to teach finances to students, so this is our duty as parentsm to educate our children financially. We are responsible for preparing our children mentally, emotionally and financially for the life that lies ahead of them. If we dont take up the task then who will? Right.

To our young readers, this is important for you because the earlier you understand the process the better off you are. Take the time to shop around for the best banks that will accommodate your financial needs. You will grow with your bank over the years and strengthen your relationship. This will allow for you to do business with your bank when the time is right. Then hopefully you'll be able to do the same for your children. This goes for our older and newly released readers as well. Let's promote generational wealth for our family.

CHAPTER 4

Credit

Now comes the topic that will be a huge part of your financial life until you pass on. The subject of this chapter has the potential to affect your family even after your death. Have you ever heard that it takes money to make money? Well that is true but it's not always the case. Credit is your life profile, it's a representation of your life from a financial standpoint. This report is so detailed that the reader of this report doesn't even have to meet you to know if they will or will not do business with you. This can be considered your adult report card of sorts. Credit reports are generated by 3 different bureaus and are represented by a numerical score. Each bureau generates its own credit score for you which is based on a numerical range. The higher your score the better the better your credit. These scores are a composite of past and current bills, rent/ mortgage, hospital bills, car notes, school loans, bank loans, etc. A paid off bill will boost your credit score and a default payment will lower your score.

A good credit score can be worth much more than money in the bank majority of the time. Businesses will work with you more once they examine your credit report due and a good payment history. A lot of jobs even look at credit scores now a days before they consider hiring employees. Don't be surprise if your girlfriend even wants to check your credit score before you two makes the relationship official. This credit score is your life line and you must protect it as such my friend. So, let's discuss how to build your credit up.

If you completed the last step than you have taken the first step towards building credit. Matter of fact, you couldn't even apply for housing or a loan without at least finishing the last and setting up a bank account. So once you have successfully kept a positive bank account for at least six months, you will began to receive credit applications. You'll receive mail to apply for credit cards, loans, furniture store credit, etc. Don't get paranoid because this is actually great news. Don't become so overly excited that you begin to apply to every application that you recieve.

A lot of people become afraid or cautious of using credit and they refuse to exercise one of their best financial tools available. These people like to believe that credit goes hand and hand with debt, and for the most part they are correct. Credit and debt are of the same cloth but understand that it is the fear of debt that is the true problem. Debt isn't meant to be feared because when used properly it is an important tool in building your credit. As in any financial matter, you must learn to manage your debt. Let's talk about some basic methods now, then we will discuss more advanced methods in the resources section in the back of the book..

Let's start with these credit card applications. There are countless credit cards but the companies have been the same for decades. So, if you build a relationship with one such as Mastercard, American Express, Apex, Capital One, Visa, etc. you have indeed made an profitable decision because all of thm communicate with each other through your credit report. So if you have a good payment history with one, you will eventually be qualified for another.

Once you choose a credit card company now it's time to choose the right card. Each card has different features that are designated for specific types of users. There are cards for young adults, students, for building credit, business, etc. If this is your first credit card, you will have to go through a rather lengthy application. This application will require a security question to verify that it is you that is applying. These security questions come from your credit report and are answers that only you should know. Most companies usually approve your application within an hour of a completed application but it could posiible take a few days..

Now that you're approved,it's time to get to the fun. Most credit cards will grant a initial credit balance of anywhere between $300.00 - $500.00. This is the norm but I know that this is not a huge balance of credit, but we will fix this. The key to boosting your credit is to successfully use your credit and pay off the balance. Since credit cards successfully operate by lending their credit to cardholders and in return they charge interest rates on the balance. This is the key to building your credit with them. You must produce a great payment history with the credit issuer.

Start by using your credit card for small purchases that you'll be able pay off almost immediately such as; gas purchases, fast food/restaurant, convenient store, etc. These small purchases won't take much to pay in full but that's sort of the point. For example, one month you will use your card twice to fill up your gas tank. Say that the sum of these transactions combine for $65.00. If your credit card bill is due next month on the 10th, then pay your balance in full two days earlier than the due date on the 8th instead.

For the first few months, you are to continue to pay off these small purchases monthly and early. Now, it's time to up the ante by making bigger purchases. The key to this is to max out your card with a purchase that you will be able to pay back earlier than the due date. You can do this by paying for items that you usually use cash for with your credit card. Then you take the cash to pay your credit card bill early. If you don't have the cash to make a purchase or the lack of something to buy then ask a friend for help. They can give you the cash for a purchase that they are planning to make and you can buy it with your credit card. Viola!

Once you continue this process for about 3 to 6 months then it is to upgrade.This si the plan, you will now call the credit card company to request an approval for a bigger credit balance. This should plan should be success in this instantance due to process that we've aleady completed. If fo some reason you are not approved then continue the process for 2 to 3 months more then try again. They'll approve the new balance and you'll complete the process again and again until you are upgraded to better new card with a larger credit balance. This new card will be exclusive and will provide better features. Guess what next? You guess right, then you go through the process again.

During this entire process your credit score will be raising through the roof. Every time you make these payments ahead of time it will strengthen your positive marks. The more positive marks you earn the better your score will become. During his process ,you are building a strong and valuable relationship with this credit card company. This will eventually allow yo to be approved for yet another card with a different credit card company. Then you will complete this process again thourghly with this new credit card company. This will eventually result in you gaining A-1 credit!

If you didn't get approved for the credit card, don't worry because there is always more than one way to accomplish your goals. You can apply for a secured prepaid card first to start your credit repair process. This will require you to deposit your personal money as an initial credit balance for the prepaid card. This means that your credit balance is secured or backed by your initial deposit. I know you are probably thinking like, "What's the point if you're using your own money?" Give me a chance and hear me out.

Secured prepaid credit card are a great to begin to build a relationship with a credit card company. Although you are using your own money, you want to treat it as if you are using their credit balance. You can accomplish by using the methods that weve previously discussed. The more you pay off the monthly fees, the higher your credit score grows. After about 3 to 6 months of completing this process, you will be approved for an official credit card. This will make this transaction more than worthwhile.

Another easy way of building your credit is through the rent to own businesses. Let's take Rent a Center for example. These businesses operate by selling you furniture, electronics, gaming systems, etc. on credit type basis. You will pick a product in which you will be able to make use of and then make a small initial payment to rent to own the product. These purchases are marked up way over market value due to the high interest rates and payment adjustments. The business will allow you to negotiatet to make weekly, bi weekly , or monthly payments in accordance with your work payment schedule.

The idea is to shop for a product that you actually are in need or want. Purchase an item that you know you will be able to pay off easily. You can shop online or inside of the store at the brick and mortar. Once you've chosen, you will complete a credit application in which you will have to verify your identity though a series of procedures. The rental place will verify your current address through a lease agreement or something similar. You will have to provide proof of employment such as check stub and your work contact information, your employer and supervisor. You will also have to provide references that will be contacted in order to vouch for you and to serve as alternate places to look for you in case you default on the payments.

If your application checks out fine, then you will be approved. Take your new Xbox One or new 50" flatscreen home and enjoy it because you are in fact buying the product. The ultimate key to this process is to keep up to date with the payments. You really want to choose a payment date that will allow for you to pay early. Remember that this business charges you by the day, so if you get paid every 2 weeks then try to get your payment due the week prior to getting paid. This allows you to prtray the illusion of you paying early. Just be sure that you can actually afford the payments.

After paying ahead of time for a few months, it is time to

speed up the process. Most of all the rent to own businesses offer an payment deal of something similar to equal to price value ending payment. This means that if you pay the balance before a certain time frame, then you can pay off and own the item for a reduced price that will be close to the retail price of the item. So our goal here is to pay these scheduled payments early if possible but most definitely on time for this period of time. Then we will begin to pay the item off quicker by paying more money every time you make a payment until you pay the remaining balance off early.

This quick payment will aid your credit score tremendously. After paying the item off early, you now not only have a good credit history at this store but an excellent credit score. This good payment transaction will show up as a positive account on your credit report and will boost your credit score. Also this account will look very attractive when the next business pulls your credit report credit. Remember this important rule, that "what makes you smile can also make you cry." Defaulting on the payments will result in a negative mark and have a total counter productive effect.

Another form of credit building can be accessed through in store credit and gas store credit. These stores offer certain amenities to their best and most frequent customers. One of these features is in the form of in store credit. You can apply through a credit application at stores such as Home Depot, Office Depot, clothing stores, as stations, etc. This process is very similar to the previous credit building strategies. This line of credit is to be strictly used in the store that you applied for.

You can use your in store credit to buy items from the store using credit instead of the cash. Since the store is lending its own line of credit, you will pay them an interest rate fee and the purchase fee. This payment will be due on an agreed scheduled payment date. You will treat this credit as you previously accomplished with rent a center. After successfully paying off the balance, you will receive a positive mark on your credit report that will help you to be approved for future credit applications.

An added bonus is that you will be able to use this credit at these stores later on down the line when you are ready to start and fund your own business. So choose a store that will help you with your business in the future.

Applying for and recieving small loans from your bank is another form of building credit. Most banks offer small loans from $300.00 - $1000.00 for their loyal account holders. These loans can be used for a multitude of reasons, from home modifications, small business funding, to car purchases, etc. There is an approval process that you must go through where you will submit your request with a reasonable purpose for the loan funds. You must provide proof of eligibility to pay back and a copy of your plan for how youre going to pay the loan balance back. The process would be similar to the past credit application processes.

If approved the bank will provide the requested loan funds that will usually clear and post to your bank account. It is always best to apply for a loan that can be easily paid off. A little trick that works well is to withdraw the money and deposit it to another bank account. Once you do this you must not spend the money because you will use this same money that you borrowed to pay off the bank loan, but not all at once. You will use the money to pay each scheduled payment ahead of time and eventually paying more to get the full balance paid off before due schedule.

Once you have done this once you then ask for a bigger loan and complete the process again. This will extend your credit at the bank as far as you can reach it. To get the full effect you must complete this process with at least 3 banks until you max at your loan balance. If completed correctly, this will eventually give the illusion of you owning a million-dollar credit rating. So that when you are ready to start your business you can tap into these bank loans. Also this will help grant you a A-1 credit score.

If you didn't get approved initially for a small bank loan than let's, try this step. You will have to begin with a secured loan instead. This loan will be backed by your own money that will be held to your savings account. This is similar to the secured credit card process as in although you are using your money. You will treat this time on loan.

You will apply for a secured loan at least 3 banks. You will use the money from one to pay the next and so on. You will then pay the payments before schedule for at least 3 months. Then you will gradually pay more until the loan and its interest fees are paid. If you do this right and pay each off early then you will be approved the unsecured loan to start the previous process. We will also discuss as more advanced method of this process in the resources section in the back!

Conclusion

As previously stated. I was 14 when my mom helped me to open my first bank account. I quickly began to order products online and enjoy the fruits of my chores. Eventually I began to realize the power of my debit card and it's purchasing power. Over the years I have defaulted on payments and over drafted on accounts. I have built up small amounts of credit card debt and hospital bills.

This is the usual process for young adults. Most of the youngsters either lack the understanding of credit and/or lack the maturity. The knowledge takes time, and some people are grown by the time they gain the understanding. I lacked both but most of all I lacked understanding. As an adult, parent, mentor, etc., we should feel the need to help prepare the younger generations for the future financially. We should teach the youth about credit early in their lives in order to help them understand. If we fail to do so than we are failing to help society.

To the readers who have already began to make a negative impact on their credit and currently has a low credit score. There are ways to repair your credit and build your score to a good level. You could have a credit report specialist who charges anywhere between $300.00 - $1000.00 to help you repair your score. In doing this please do your due diligence to be sure that the specialist is actually credible and reliable. You do not want to waste money, nor be scammed by a con artist.

Also, you could begin to repair your credit on your own. The first step is to request your free credit report online. You will copy the information of the negative accounts on your report and paste them into a blank document. Do not dispute these accounts online; instead you will write a series of dispute letters to the three different bureaus. These letters accompanied by a copy of your identification such as, id and social security card will start the process. This will take a length of 3 – 6 months to compile but it should get the ball rolling. Be sure to conduct your own research first before you begin the credit repair process. Now let's move on to the next step.

CHAPTER 5

Car and House Ownership

I remember when I was 17 and the mother of my oldest daughter was pregnant with my child. We would argue over some of the most random issues. At the time, I was head over heels in love with her. So, this drove me to asking my uncle for relationship advice. He told me something that not only changed my view of him but also my view of relationships. Now I didn't take it for face value but I'll explain it to you.

He told me, "Nephew, the older you get, the more it'll take to get a woman and keep a woman. You're young now and the women only expect so much out of you but the older you get the harder it gets." At the time I was young and took his advice as jealousy. Jealousy over my youth, looks, my woman, etc. So, I didn't take heed of the advice and wrote it off as hate. When you're young you can be a little stubborn but it doesn't pay to be hard headed because you will eventually have to learn the hard way.

This didn't totally make sense to me until I got older and was told something similar from a guy that was something like a brother of mines. I was 23 years old and fresh out of jail where I spent 13 months. I was working as a brick mason labor with my uncle's business. I was still young if you look at age but my mother had passed when I was 19. This had caused me to grow up a lot quicker and mature. I was a man now and had to carry myself as one.

At the time I had finally found a place to stay. Initially, when

I was released I bounced around from a few places until I was threatened to become homeless. This is my worst fear in life, to be homeless. Eventually with prayer and love I got in contact with my brother and ended up moving in with him, my cousin, and two of my brother's friends that have known me all my life. It was five of us in a 3-bedroom house, not including my girlfriend who slept with me on a pallet on the front room's floor.

We all worked together and got paid at the same time. The difference was how each of us chose to spend our money . Most of the guys tricked their money off and by Monday they were broke, but not Rim. Rim was my brother's friend who had known me since I was 5 years old and for that he had been like a brother to me. Rim wouldn't spend a lot of money on drugs, whores and alcohol but he tended to handle the important things first and stick to a budget. This intrigued me because by Monday everybody else had to borrow money for cigarettes and lunch.

So, one Friday night, Rim and I drank a few beers and talked about random subjects. We somehow got on the subject of money and how to handle it properly. He said, "There are three things a man needs in order to be a man and that's a job, a car and his own place." Over the years I added to this with the possesion of your own cell phone. As far as I was concerned this was an honest and true doctrine, and this further cemented the fact that my uncle had stated 4 years ago.

Without a job a man cannot provide money in which he needs to take care of himself and his family. How can a man conduct business or be in place when he needs to without a phone? A man needs a car in order to safely and timely get himself and/or family to somewhere. A grown man has not fully grown until he can support his own home. This doesn't just go for men but for women as well who strive to be independent. So now that we've discussed this how lets discuss proper ownership.

Let's start with the least of the rule, which is owning your own cell phone. For credit purposes, I am discussing this because buying a cell phone can affect your credit score. The prices of these phones are so high that they are considered to extremely valuable property. Unless you are buying a phone that isn't of any quality, most phone companies require a credit check in order to lease a new cell phone.

Most cellphone companies such as Sprint, T-Mobile, ATT, Verizon, etc. allow payment plans for phones. Say that you are interested in buying the new Galaxy foldable or Apple iPhone. Once you begin to check out either online or in store, the company will request to view your credit report. If your credit history is sufficient, they can allow you to purchase the phone for as low as $0.00 down or for a small deposit. If your credit score isn't high enough, they'll require you to pay a little more down on the deposit or if the score is real low you'll have to pay the entire retail price for the cell phone. If you took the previous credit steps then you'll be approved.

Once approved, you may be required to pay for shipping and handling and/or first month's cell phone bill. Your credit is the deciding factor in to generating how much your final payment at check out will be. If you are not required to pay anything at all then that's a good sign for your credit. Most of the time that only means everything but the deposit will be due on your first bill. You should take the time to understand all fees associated with your account so that you can better assess your first bill. This bill will include your phone plan that you chose during the purchase of your phone. Also be prepared to begin paying for your new cell phone. Each bill will consist of a monthly payment of the cell phone towards paying off the overall balance.

As you begin to pay the bill more and more, you will notice various fees occurring. These are fees that you have to be conscience of because they can take you by surprise which will produce an confusing cell phone bill. This process acts as any normal rent to own situation works, where once the phone is paid off and the account is in good standing your credit score will be positively affected. This will be a very generous mark for your credit score and will qualify you to apply for all type of services such as; other cell phones, Wi-Fi services, cable services, etc. All these services are rather trivial, but each service can add to your credit score and each service usually requires a credit report check.

You could always take a more affordable route when cell phone shopping. There are countless cellphone shops the deal in used items. The technicians at these business usually but used products to refurbish the devices. After refurbishing the items and getting them to run smoothly, they will present the devices for sale either in store or online. These phones are most certainly the best deal when you want to buy an quality phone for an affordable price.

Now let's discuss transportation, which is extremely important. Any adult isn't complete without owning their own personal transportation. Time is our friend but it can also become our enemy because time wasted is nonrefundable. So, every chance you get be sure to make sure your time is being used productively. The best way to accomplish this is through purchasing your own personal transportation. If you have a job interview coming up, you don't want to risk being late bycatching the bus or relying on a family member or friend to take you. You want to get to and from work as safe and expedient as possible.

A car or truck is best for these moments of tight schedules, I want to let you know that its more than one way to acquire this transportation, and I will start with the cheaper route. There are always used cars on the market that are great for your type of transportation needs. You don't have to necessarily purchase a car with a note in order to get back and forth to work or school. To be honest, I wouldn't recommend getting a car note in the beginning of your financial process. You do not need another bill to pay, you need more money save and invest.

I know you heard countless stories of people dropping $3000.00 - $5000.00 only to buy a lemon or a car that has a lot of mechanical issues. This is ugly truth that can happen if you don't conduct your due diligence when car shopping. There are countless websites that you can go to where owners and dealers advertise their cars for reasonable prices. So, let's discuss a few of them now, some of which are my favorites.

Let's start with one of the original peers to peer forums, Craigslist. Craigslist and forums like it are used for owners to advertise their items that they own for sale. You can go to the tab that is labeled cars and trucks for sale, either by owner or dealer. Once there you can specify the car you want by make, model, year, etc. Best of all you can choose a price range in order to narrow your search down to a range you can afford.

You want to be aware of any scams on those sites because some posts can be fraudulant and can harm you in a majority of ways. Let's discuss some ways to weed out the fakes. Try to stick with cars that have realistic pictures and there should be multiple pictures of the vehicle.. You should be able to discern if the person has taken the picture themselves or used an photo off the internet. Remember, if it sounds too good to be true then it probably is too good to be true. If you see a car worth $10,000.00 for $4500.00 than it is probably a scam or a lemon. One last thing, pay attention to the contact information, if it's a weird number or just an email address it could be a fake. Although some people will have different area codes and some would rather use email than post at their personal phone number. If you do contact the seller, then please proceed with caution.

Once you contact a seller it is time to schedule a visit to see the vehicle. Be sure to meet up in safe locations within the safer time frames of day. You can never be too cautious but if the seller agrees to these conditions then he/she is probably legit. If you're not a mechanic and you don't know a whole lot about cars, then I suggest you bring along someone who is knowledgeable of mechanics. If you don't know somebody personally then you can always offer a few dollars to a mechanic to look at it before you buy. This will help to weed out any lemons and to help calculate if there will be future mechanical issues.

If everything checks out then it's almost time to buy. You should be sure to check the title to make sure it's clean. Don't buy a car that the title has a "lein" on it due to a title loan or if the title isn't even issued in the owner's name. Don't buy a car without a title because it'll be rather complicated to complete the purchase and to transfer ownership. You must obtain some good car insurance and the tag for your car as soon as possible. You don't want to get the car towed and impounded because that can be very expensive.

There are other apps and websites that offer car sales as well. One being the Facebook marketplace, which is a good place to shop for a used car. Just be sure to follow the safety procedures expressed in the previous few paragraphs as to not get dupped. Apps like Autotrader, Carvana, Car Max, etc. offers online car sales. These businesses may also deliver as well for a delivery and handling fee. These sites are more professional than the forums but I still recommend doing your due diligence before purchasing a car.

If you don't have a lot of time to do a lot of car shopping or aren't good with searching, then have the sellers come to you. This is a little trick I've been doing since I was in my early 20's. On those forum sites such as Craigslist and Marketplace you will post your own ad listing on the forum. This listing will consist of you explaining your need for a decent car that is up and running. You will then list a price range you're comfortable with. Be sure that this price isn't too high or too low. You don't want to attract the wrong cars but leave some room to negotiate. Also you want to place your contact information within the text so that the user can easily see instead of searching for it. A phone number is best because it's the easiest form of communication. You could always download a phone app like text now to use an anonymous phone number instead of providing your personal number. Thank me later.

Your other option is to lease or rent to own a car. This is the more expensive of the options but usually the more popular. There are two types of cars you can pay a car note on and that's used cars and new cars. I recommend at the beginning of your journey to lease a used car because you could pay this car off more quickly than a new model car. They both usually require the same application conditions with the only differences is between the price and the credit score.

In order to lease these cars, you will need to provide a few qualifications. First and most of all you'll need proof of income. This can be a copy of your paycheck stub from your job and/or transaction history of your bank accounts that shows the deposits. This is where your bank account and direct deposit come in handy. You'll need proof of your address and of course a driving license. Once you've established these requirements you'll need to pass a credit check.

Your credit check relies upon what kind of car you looking to purchase. Of course, a used car won't need as great of a credit score as a new model car. The better the credit score, the better the car, and the better selections of cars that you qualify for. Once you've got a few cars selected it's time to test drive the main selections, then it si time to talk numbers.

Most of these cars will require a down payment to drive off. The down payment is considered to be a trust measure between the car company and you in order for the seller to receive a good portion of their initial investment back upfront. I bet you can pretty much guess how the deposit amount is reached? You guessed it, your credit is the key, so I bet youre beginning to see the importance of a good credit score. The better the credit score the less the down payment and sometimes you'll pay $0.00 down if your credit is that good.

Also the better your credit score the lower your monthly payment. So once you agree to your new terms and conditions be sure to opt for a warranty. A good warranty will give you at least 15-30 days to bring your car back to trade in, get your refund and/or get your car fixed if there are immediate mechanical issues. This is an important feature to get so that you won't buy a car that will quit on you within a month. Also, negotiate for a monthly payment that benefits your pay schedule. You want to be able to pay this bill on time and early. If it is a used car then you want to pay extra on some payments in order to pay the car off quickly.

The newer the car, the longer it'll take you to pay off. Don't get me wrong, there's nothing wrong with buying a car brand new. It's just not a good idea to add such a lengthy and huge bill to your finances when you are in the beginning stages of accomplishing your goals. One of the reasons is that cars tend to depreciate in value over the years, unless the car is a limited edition, vintage edition or a collector's edition. In fact, the car will immediately lose value as soon as you drive off the car lot. The best advice I can give you is to never attempt to live beyond your means because it can drive you into poverty and debt. With that said, let's discuss housing.

Real estate is a market that will be around and essential for decades to come. Housing is something that everyone will need regardless. This is an asset that proves to be detrimental not only for yourself but also in regards to your life and health as well. Purchasing or renting a property with the right housing conditions can be difficult and down right expensive. Don't worry because we will discuss some purchasing methods that can assist you.

Most young adults choose apartments for their first housing situation. Apartments are attractive because of their accessibility, cheap rent, less utility bills and they just do not come with much of a commitment. For a young adult who doesn't really want to commit to a property, then these apartments can be great. The problems begin to form when yourealize that your privacy, money, rights, etc are being comprimised. Once you understand these issues then you will begin to realize that apartments are not that desirable pertaining to the journey of your goal accomplishing.

First, let's discuss an issue that can be a huge factor for anybody, young or older. Apartments and other multi-unit housing lose a lot of points in the privacy factor. Due to the amount of neighbors that you will undoubtedly have in an apartment complex, your business is everybody's business. Due to the commercial construction of most complexes, the quality of materials is sacrificed. Most apartments I have been in have walls so thin that you can hear your neighbor's conversations, music being blasted, kids running and jumping on the floor, etc. This can prove to be a bit much when you need some peace and serenity.

Your rights in regards to the apartment are quite limited due to your temporary ownership. The property management team has ultimate jurisdiction over the apartments. They hold the right to enter your apartment at any time, although they tend to be reasonable. This can be testy if you are not comfortable with a group of somewhat strangers coming into your home at any given time. Most apartments have restrictions on personalization effects such as; decorating, pets, cable providers. How many people that you are allowed to have over, etc.?

Most apartments will only allow you to decorate your home to specify degrees. You can't just up and decide that you want to change the color of your bedroom at any time you want. You'll have to put in a request and more than likely if it is approved the money will come out of your pocket by being added on to your monthly rent. You can't hang up pictures with nails because any holes that you hammer in to the wall will be considered as property damage. All the changes will have to be approved through the apartment property management.

If you have pets then you'll have to find a pet-friendly apartment building. There are a lot of apartments that are pet friendly but they do require more money. You will undoubtedly have to pay a higher deposit to cover any damage that your pet may cause during the stay. More than likely you'll have to pay a monthly pet fee that'll be tacked on to the monthly payment.

Some apartments limit you to certain cable and internet service providers as well. If you have good standing relationship with a certain CSP/ISP, want to try a different provider, or if you have just plain found a new one that you want to use, then this could be an issue. Some apartment complexes have contracts with certain providers and restrict use to only this provider. A lot of the time, their problem is related to drilling holes into the walls because some cable companies will have to do this to network. This can conflict with the destruction of property rule. Alot of these cable and internet providers now install wireless cable and modem hardware.

 Apartments usually have restrictions on how many people that a occupant can have staying in an apartment at one time. Some even restrict how many visitors that you can have visit the apartment at one time. The apartment's property mangement can evict you for breaking these number rules because they are usually noted in the rental contract that you were to read and sign. Apartments will want to know what adults will be living there with you and their information for safety and financial purposes.

 Speaking of financial reasoning, apartments are money pits. I say this for a good reason, you will never be able to completely own the apartment that you rent. Therefore it is basically a liability that takes from you, and although it provides you shelter, the apartment will never be yours for you to do as you please. With that said, you could be staying at an apartment 5 years and suddenly you begin to come up on hard times. It doesn't matter how long you've been living there and payimg your rent on time, they will still evict you, business is business. I know that this situation can happen with a house as well but within 5 years of making payments on time, you could rent to own the house with the staregies that we will discuss..

 So, let's begin with the biggest investment that most adults will acquire in their lifetime, purchasing and owning your first house. To be honest you do have the option of renting the house but I feel as if that would be a waste of time and money when you could rent to own the property. The first house that you own is a huge investment, because of the equity at stake in its ownership. A house is almost as liquidable as money in the bank because you can use your house to boorw money through it at any given time by borrowing against the equity. Now I will not be getting too in-depth with real estate because that is a subject for a separate book in itself, but I will discuss some of the major details.

 First, let's discuss the process of discovering a good house to rent to own. You can find a lot of these type of houses through online forums like Craigslist and through various online websites that deal in thiese matters. You'll conduct your search on these sites with similar procedures that you would use when you were buying your car. The difference is that if you are to be scammed here then you'll be risking a greater amount of money than before. So be careful and be motivated when commiting your due dilligence research. Just remember that rent to own houses are a high commodity in the market because they are very asset valuable.

You may also find a lot of these houses through a google search by looking for rent-to-own houses in your area. When you do this search you will be directed to a high number of websites. A lot of these sites offer apps for your mobile devices. Some of the best apps are Realtor.com, Zillow and Homefinder.com. Using these sites, you can really specify your search to tune your needs.

I truly prefer to buy the houses directly from the owner of the property. This is how you will find the best deals because there is no middle man dicatating the neogitiation. To accomplish this acquisition you will have to have a bit of knowledge or experience with house maintenance or at least know some people who do. You will need to be able to evaluate the house for any damages that need to be fixed that will drive the price down for you. Also, you don't want to buy a house that isn't worth the price or will be inhabitable within the next few years.

Most owners/sellers who are looking to rent to own will want to have a sizable down payment of goodwill up front to initiate the buying process. This deposit will be a portion of the overall price that is meant to provide the seller with good faith moving forward. Usually, the down payment will be 10% of the overall price. The monthly rent payments would usually be 5% of the overall price. These houses are usually cash payments due to the process of how you acquired it.

A lot of the rent to own houses are usually sold as is. This means that the responsibility is upon the renter to fix the house up. Some owners would still like to play a big part in the renovation of the house, but most give the reigns over to the buyer. I know this can be rather costly but remember this is considered to be a investment. The money you pay for the deposit on the front end will be applied to the overall payment on the back end. So the money that you will put into the property to bring the property up to market standards will boost the value of the property. Therefore, this will be money well spent.

I want to give you some advice that I learned the hard way. Back in the year 2015, I was engaged to be married to the mother of my newborn daughter. At the time my brother and I were sharing the expenses of renting a house together. It was a three-bedroom and 1 bath. My brother and his girlfriend had their own room and my fiancé, my daughter and I had our own room. The third room was vacant but wasn't to be used. Needless to say, the house was cramped.

Eventually, the company that my brother and sister-in-law brought to the house was beginning to become unsafe for my growing family. So I found a house that was big enough and affordable for my budding family. It was a two-bedroom and 1 bath. The previous owner was an older woman who had passed away in the house. She was also a chronic hoarder because she collected a good amount of newspapers, trash, old magazines and clothes. Needless to say that the house was in need of some work before it could be habitable.

So, I worked a deal out with the new owner of the property who was renting out the house to me, the son of the older woman, in order to work on the house to waive the deposit fee. For two and a half weeks I cleaned that house up before I even felt comfortable showing it to my fiancé. So once the house was finally livable, we all decided to meet officially. So that weekend my family and I met with the owner and his family for the first time.

Immediately the older couple fell in love with my daughter who was just an arm baby during this time. They met my young and beautiful fiancé and they were charmed. It was as if they were meeting me for the first time. They saw me as the young family man who was on the path of being successful and they were intrigued.

That was the day the owner pulled me to the side and made me an very interesting offer. He told me that he had spoken with his wife and they were so pleased to discover these circumstances.

They had decided to offer me the house as a rent-to-own home. I was excited and quickly agreed because it was a great opportunity for the young family that we were. I was so anxious that when I got the paperwork from them that I didnt even look it over, I just signed it.

Over the next few months, my fiancé and I lived together in the house while we redecorated and enjoyed our new old home. We were young and we were inexperienced with being in a serious relationship. Over the next few months, there were a few problems that we had that eventually became too much to bear. We split up and I continued to stay at the house by myself.

Eventually, I began to live like a bachelor and started to let loose. I would have my friends over and I constantly had various women over to the house. Eventually, my home habits got back to the owner and he was very upset. To be honest, I felt that there wasn't anything that he could do about it, but the owner was adamant in telling me that he would evict me. I didn't understand how he felt so confident until he showed me the original housing contract that I signed.

The paper that I thought was a rent-to-own agreement was nothing more than a complicated rental application. Through all the fuss of renovating and rushing I failed to even look at the paper to examine it. This was my foot in the door and I knew it but I celebrated prematurely. I felt so dumb for not taking the time to read the contract. It was nothing I could do about it that I knew of it, so I just gave up and gave in.

The point of this story, but I believe that you have already figured it out, is to always make sure your paper work is legit. Take the time to read every line on those papers that apply to your rights and obligations. If you are not skilled in reading and understanding contractual agreements, then hire someone more experienced to take a look at it. This is the most important part and it is the equivalent to your lifeline. You don't want to be tricked out of our money, only to be thrown out on the streets.

Let's discuss another option for first-time home buyers and this process consists of buying the property with your credit. If when you are searching for houses you happen to run across some houses for sale that are of good condition but they want a good amount of money for it. Don't worry because they can still be purchased through your credit. Especially if you've used the financial process that I provided in the chaters leading up to this point.

You will first contact the sellers, who more than likely will enlist the services of a licensed realtor. The realtor is the middleman or salesman who earns a fee in the form of a commission when he/she successfully sells the home. The plan is to view the house, evaluate the house, assess the house, and make a offer relying on the amount of repairs that the property needs. If you both reach a price in which you both agree to then you'll begin the closing and escrow process.

During this process, you have up to 60 days to complete the purchase and closing of the property. This is the part when you must speak to the mortgage broker at the bank(s) that your account is with. You will fill out an application to aplly for a loan in order to buy the home. While the bank is processing your application, they will send their own professionals to assess the property to determine if the property is worth the price. This along with a credit check, employment check, and reference check will determine if your application is approved.

If everything checks out then the bank will approve you for a home equity line of credit, H.E.L.O.C. and/or mortgage. The HELOC means that the bank will buy the house from the seller in your name through the bank. The bank will own a percentage of the equity in the house, and you will pay the bank monthly payments. The monthly payment will usually be 5% of the overall price of the property. The payments will go towards you completely owning the property out right and once you're finished paying the overall balance then the deed and the property becomes yours.

The thing about owning a house is that it is similar to having money available in the bank. At any given moment, you can go to your bank in order to borrow some more money in exchange for more equity. Although if you default on payments then your house will be foreclosed on and you'll lose the house. So be sure to have a good plan if you choose borrow against your house. This is good if you need some seed money for a business venture or investment strategy. Just be cautious when dealing with your living arrangements. For more real estate advice check the resource section in the back.

Section 2

(Education) Introduction.

As you probably already can guess, education is very important to me and it is essential to your plan of success. Since birth, we are programmed to be curious of our surroundings and to learn about everything possible. Have you ever witnessed how a baby can be fascinated by everything and tend to imitate the people that they are around? We are meant to be this way throughout our entire lives because the gift of learning never ends.

There are no age restrictions on education and there is no limit to how much you can learn. My ex-mother-in-law is 58 years old and to this day she is attending college to earn a master's degree in her field of choice. This surprised me until I went to college and shared a class with a 70-year-old woman who was in th process of earning herself a business degree. This is a way of life, this is our right as humans to be able to progress. To progress you must have some form of education and you must continue learn throughout your life.

Many of the young readers grew up in a community where most of the older people that were around you were not very supportive of school. Some of you grew up in a household where if or when you graduated you would be the first family member with a High School Diploma. Well, I am here to tell you that you can accomplish this goal and much more. Don't ever limit yourself to what you can and cannot do because the sky is the limit.

Do not get me wrong, there are plenty of people who have succeeded in life without the completion of a formal education. What I am telling you is that you do need some type of education to become successful whether it's formal or informal. So, if you do realize that continuing formal education isn't right for you and you want to choose another path there are plenty of alternative options that we will discuss in this section, my favorite section.

As you read this section, I want you to be open-minded to the ideas and different choices that we wil discuss. This isn't a one size fit all kind of thing, so everyone's education plan will be different. I want you to choose a path that is best tailored to your strengths and your needs. Although I don't discuss every education path, I do discuss the paths that I am familiar with. Be sure to take up your own research as well to be sure you are choosing the right path because education is very important and so is your time.

CHAPTER 6

Ged/High school Diploma

We're going to start off with arguably. The most important of the educational diplomas. The High School Diploma/G.E.D is the first major diploma that a young adult will receive. This is what all the elementary classes and middle school graduations were leading up to. These are two of the most esential diplomas for being able to apply to job applications currently. In most cases, if you're an adult without a high school diploma or GED, even the local neighborhood McDonald's won't hire you. Isn't that a shame of all shames, not to discredit McDonalds as an employer.

I realize that at this time the young readers probably aren't well versed into planning their future to realize how important this diploma is. I also understand that if you are reading this, then you do have the will to plan for your life. For this I applaud you because it is a blessing to be mature enough at a young age to actually prepare for your future. Bravo!

This diploma is your passage into adulthood. To employers this is framed proof that you have went through required training in order to begin the next stage of life. For most of you this is an accomplishment that is huge. Because for some of you will be the first in your household to earn one of these degrees. Whether this is you or not this is still a great accomplishment to be very proud of, and you should be proud.

One thing I must advise you of is to never take this time of your life for granted. Your high school years are the most important years of your youth and should be treated as such. Take the time to enjoy your growth and your day-to-day schedule of high school. This will be the most memorable time of your life but also the most carefree. I must admit that after this part of your life it is time for the real world. High school is your preparation for this real world of life.

Let's begin with the most obvious, and that is earning good grades. Your grades are recorded throughout your entire school life. So I know that you can see how important these grades are in your path of life. Each semester you have a report card and with each semester comes a composite score of your grades. This composite is called your G.P.A. or grade point average. After each school year, you are given a composite GPA for that year. This GPA will follow you throughout your adult life.

When you do graduate from high school your GPA is your overall grade for your entire school life. The higher your GPA the better you are received due to your education. It's like a user rating for a business listed on Google, so strive to earn 5 stars. This GPA is one of the most important factors that colleges will view in order to decide to accept you in to their establishment. We will discuss the other factors throughout this chapter.

Some jobs will even ask for your GPA when applying on their applications. They want to know how well you are "rated" in receiving and processing information. That's crazy huh? A job wants to know how good your grades were because starting a new job requires quite a bit of learning. Your future employer wants to be confident in the fact that you are good at learning and will learn the position you are applying for quickly.

Electives may not seem as important to an academic student but believe me, they are very important. Electives are the classes that tend to expand past the norm of academia. These classes usually teach students life skills that will aid them into adulthood. Each of these classes focuses on different qualities and strengths.

Sports/Gym is an elective that most can't see the benefit from but it teaches a lot of qualites to the students. This elective not only promotes physical health and activeness, but it also generates other qualities. Leadership is one of the main qualities for the world that is filled with more than enough followers. We need more reliable leaders. This also teaches a healthy amount of competitiveness so that we as a people can prosper. Although, these are only two qualities.

Debate class/Public speaking is an elective that academic students can appreciate. There are other classes that are similar to this elective such as student government, socialism, etc. These electives are meant to inspire a healthy amount of competition that will help mold our youth into the future of our society. They give them the tools needed to be able to command a presence and to gain the attention of their subjects. All the while alluring them into their positions with persuading language and relatable.

Electives such as home economics, agriculture and workshops are almost extinct in our high schools, but why? These classes teach youth how to survive life as an adult, whether it's how to cook a decent meal and learning to clean after yourself; or how to build your own dining room table or plaster a hole in your wall. These electives are your guide to living on your own or providing a service to your household.

What some fail to realize is that these electives are a source of aid when applying the qualities later on in your life. Colleges take electives into consideration when they are looking over admittance applications. Electives like public speaking and debate groups look great when you're applying with a major that relates. Student government will help if you're into politics of course, and JROTC will help you to gain rank if you decide to join the military. Imagine how effective taking agriculture or shop will take you if you want to work with your hands. The opportunities are limitless so don't underestimate the importance of these classes.

If high school is not necessarily working out for you then there is an alternative to the high school diploma. The G.E.D. or general equivalency diploma is widely considered as an equal substitute for the high school diploma. Some even consider it to be more difficult to obtain a GED than the HSD considering what grade you previously dropped out at and how long since you have been to school. To earn this diploma you must pass an exam that will summarize all the major subjects of your high school academics. The thing about this is that the exam is said to become more difficult each year.

I was 17 years old when I finally realized that high school wasn't going to work for me and that I was in need of a different route. I grew up with a rebellious attitude towards authority and hatred for being told what to do. When I was in the 8th grade I got into a physical altercation with the assistant principal of my middle school. I was immediately expelled to attend the alternative school of my school distinct. It wasn't all bad but it wasn't all good either.

After my semester was over with in the alternative school, I was allowed to go back to high school, in which I attended a school out of my district. I excelled there as well through academics and became quite popular. I eventually tried out for the basketball team because I felt that I was good and I truly loved the sport. During an after-school practice, I took offense at a student and drained a 3 pointer. As I was coming back down from the jump shot my shorts fell into a sag.

Due to the school gym's rule of "no sagging" the coach instantly jumped to scream for me to get out of the gym. I don't know if it was because I had been dating a girl on the basketball team and the fact that she was there or if it was just my rebellious attitude. It was probably a mixture of both with the presence of my girlfriend tipping towards failure. I began to cuss the coach out with a barrage of vulgar language while threatening him. Needless to say, I wasn't allowed back in the gym. Although, I didn't get expelled due to the belligerent role the coach played.

The next school year I attended the high school in my district to join my original student body class. I was back with the people I grew up with through school. This is the year that I met the mother of my daughter and I instantly fell for her. So, one day I was walking her to class, reading her a poem that I had wrote for her and the assistant principal screamed at me to tuck my shirt in. There was a rule in our schools that required that we tuck all shirts in except for sweaters or jerseys. I was wearing a throwback Jordan jersey this particular day.

This principal had been on my case the whole school year and finally, after a good period of this negativityI had finally figured out the reason why. The first reason was because he read my school file and he was pissed that I had been in a physical altercation with an assistant principal in my 8th grade school year. Second, he found out that I was the son of a former basketball teammate of his from college. This wouldve been fine except the fact that my dad had stolen his girlfriend back in college. To be honest I can't blame him for not liking me because I had an extremely cocky attitude as well.

So, when he screamed at me, I proceeded to ignore him and walk my girlfriend to class. He took this as a sign of the utmost disrespect. When I tried to walk past him, he grabbed my jersey and I turned to him and gave him a 3-piece combo that I know didn't faze him. He was every bit of 6'4 and 300 lbs. and I was 6'0 and a mere 190 pounds at that. He showed a great amount of restraint when he chose to expel me rather than to pummel me.

Once again I was kicked out of the school district again but this time it was my last. I was blessed to have parents who had a decent amount of cash flow because my only option was to attend a private school. I can tell you now that I instantly realized that I didn't fit in with the students at this school. These kids were raised in a household with generous amounts of cash flow and parents with excellent careers. It seemed as if everybody had cars and Jordans. Although I came from a great family, I still had to hustle to get the name brand clothing that I wanted to wear.

So one day I had decided to bring a gun to school to sell to one of my friends. I thought I was very conspicuous with everything, but word had got out quickly. My friend planned to give me the money after the 3rd block. So I went to my 2nd class of the day which was a nice paced class that I actually enjoyed. All this time I had the weapon concealed in my hack pack.

There was this girl in the class who I hadn't really noticed that she had a crush on me. This particular day she let her interest be known for everyone to see. The teacher paired us up in twos to work on an assignment. This young lady and I begin to hit it off and laugh throughout the class. We were flirting in front of the entire class. We attended lunch on this particular block and we sat together and ate.

I was new to this school and didn't realize that she already had a boyfriend that was actually one of the stars of the basketball team. After the bell rang ending this class, he met us at the door. He must have heard about the flirting because not only was this guy mad, but he was huge. He confronted me in front of everyone and my response was quick and dumb. I threatened to use the weapon on him. He was in disbelief but shocked when someone whispered to him that I did in fact have a weapon on me, so he backed down. Are we noticing a trend beginning to form?

The next class I was able to sell the gun to my friend. He then left school early and it was just in time. I was called to the principal's office because the boyfriend had told a staff member that I had a weapon. When he searched my bag he only found a liquor bottle. He escorted me to the dumpster to throw away the bottle. Due to my high-grade point average and potential, he decided not to suspend me but chose to speak with my mother in a meeting.

The night before the meeting I stayed up all night long thinking about my future. I realized that I had been constantly making the same mistakes because I wasn't on my right path. I knew I needed a change. So, the next day at the meeting the principal told my mother what happened and explained that due to the outcome and my potential he wouldn't expel me. My mother was relieved but I wasn't. So I expressed my thoughts to them.

I told them both that I had come to the realization that high school wasn't the right path for me. Although I kept attempting to conquer this path I constantly hit a brick wall. This always caused me to repeat the same mistakes that led me to this point that I was at now. So I told them I wanted to drop out of school to attend Job Corps and earn my GED.

There are many places that are available to young adults who are in the transition from high school to adulthood. These institutions are established in order to teach tools needed to provide for yourself in the world. The rules are much more lenient which allows a person more freedom to make decisions on their own. That's the point that stood out to me because of the lack of overbearing authority figures literally hanging over our shouldesr. Now don't get it wrong because there are always going to be authority figures on any level of life and these facilities grant you a certain level of freedom to be an adult. We're going to discuss few of these now.

Let's start with the one I attended and enjoyed; Job Corp. Job Corp will always have a special place in my heart. They have a great academic model that has inspired me throughout the years. They offer a multitude of tools to help mold you but also they provide you with a great amount of recreation. Not to mention the food was delicious when I attended and that was a plus.

Once you choose a location that you want to attend they will provide you with the transportation to the campus. From the moment you get on that bus and wave fairwell to your family, you will feel overcomed with a feeling of independence. This feeling can be scary at first to the same but this is inevitable because adulthood and independence go hand and hand.

Understand you are not alone on this journey. Look around you, there are other young adults with you on this path and they are feeling the same way as you. To truly solidify your band some of these guys will become your OT brothers and sisters. The other members will accompany you throughout your journey at Job Corp. So, you guys will have a bond that will gel together from the very beginning. So you will usually have a good support system when you arrive at the campus.

Once you touchdown and begin to go through the new arrival process where they speak with you quickly and check your belongings for drugs, weapons, etc. you are assigned to a dorm and a room. These rooms will house anywhere between 4-8 people. Not to worry because you'll be out and about most of the time handling your business and enjoying yourself. So introduce yourself to your roommates, then get you some rest because you have a busy week ahead of you.

The first week you will go through an orientation which is much like a tour of the facility. You and your OT brothers and sisters will be guided through the campus while filling out paperwork for administration purposes. This is the time you will make some decisions about your path.

If you haven't earned an HSD or GED yet. You will be given an opportunity here at this campus. You will first be given an entry level assessment in order to determine your current education level. If you don't score high enough, they'll assign you to study classes according to how you scored on each subject on your assessment. At this point, you could choose to earn an HSD or a GED. If you score high enough you'll be set up for a pre-GED test and then the GED Test itself.

Job Corps offers trade programs that will train you within the field of your choice in order to prepare you for employment. During orientation, you will be introduced to each program's class and teacher briefly. After being introduced to each you will be asked to choose a minimum of 3 trades you're interested in. The next week you will sit in on each program's class for a day each. You will then be prompted to pick the trade that you will want to learn.

The great thing about those programs that Job corps offer is that they are all certified through the government. Which mean that you can take these certifications anywhere and they will be validated. Once you completed the GED/ HSD you'll be offered a scholarship to college depending on how high you scored. After completing the trade program. Job Corps usually works with businesses in order to offer you employment if you were exceptional in your program.

There are monetary incentives as well. Once you complete your academic program, they grant you a certain amount of a cash incentive for the trade program. That's great, isn't it? Every month they will disperse funds for hygiene and other personal products. They will also provide transportation to the store to buy said products.

TIME MANIPULATION: THE 24/8 MINDSET

Recreation is great in your downtime for when you want to chill after classes to read or interact with others. Most campuses house a multitude of places to do just this such as; a game room, theater on campus, outside gazebos, gyms, and lounge areas. They offer different sports as well if you're an athlete where you compete against other job corps. Once a week they host a dance for the campus to relieve some stress with music and dance moves. Finally, students eat 3 times a day with a snack at night, sounds great right?

If you are not comfortable with moving from home, there are alternate paths for your situation. There are programs that offer GED practice and testing. These classes will usually vary regarding the schedule for adults who have kids and/or have to work. They classes are taught by accredited instructors that are certified through the government. Some of these programs offer a cash incentive for passing the test. I mean if you're going to earn the degree then you might as well get paid while earning it.

Once you have your HSD or CED there are plenty of vocational programs that operate throughout the areas. These programs usually are a extension of high schools and some are operated by non-profit organizations. There are a multitude of trades offered through these programs, mostly taught by masters of the field who have gained success and experience that they are willing to share with you. Usually, these programs cost a small fee of anywhere between $35-$100 but the knowledge you gain is invaluable.

I couldn't stress to you enough how important these certificates are for your life plan to be successful. The GED/HSD alone is worth your time and dedication in order to earn it. Please don't take these two lightly because these diplomas can truly mean the difference between a good job or a decent job. If while you're earning your diplomas you realize that you have a knack for academics then let's go to the next level, college.

CHAPTER 7

Community College/University.

    Upon gaining my GED from Job caps in 2006, I had got into some trouble at the campus and could no longer attend. I was at yet another crossroads in my life and didn't really have a plan. I only knew that the next logical step was to continue my education. I had scored so high on the GED test that I was offered a small scholarship to the local community college. I had chosen the health program in Job Corps in order to earn a certification but didn't even get the chance to attend. So I decided to go to college.

    I didn't want to go to just any college, I wanted to attend the great Jackson State University. I grew up planning to attend JSU because I loved everything about the campus. It is a historical black college in the root of a historical black city. I had the dream of joining a frat; going to frat parties; attending sports games and overall graduating as a JSU Alum.

    I told my mother my plan but as you can imagine she was distraught by my exit from Job Corps. When I told her my next venture she was surprised. She wasn't surprised that I wanted to continue my education because I was always really book smart but surprised that I had made up my mind so quickly. She saw the look of determination on my face and knew that I had made my mind up. There was only one thing left that stood in my way, taking the ACT.

    The ACT/SAT is your gateway into your college career. So yes this exam is extremely important and you should treat it as such. This next exam will test you on everything that you have or should have learned since entering school, plus some more. The test is graded on a scale of 1-36 being the highest and close to academic genius. The higher the score the better school you can attend and the less money you will have to spend to attend college through scholarships and grants.

The thing is that the closer you are out of high school the better your chances to score high due to the criteria being fresh on your mind. If you haven't been at school for a while there are classes that can tutor you to tack the ACT/SAT in order to get you back in shape. Some of those classes cost a small fee but if you were to pay, it would be well worth it. There are a multitude of books there that can help the cause and I list some in the resources that I used or if I think that it is a good brand with good study habits.

Once I studied up and took the ACT, I applied to JSU and was accepted. I began attending JSU as a Biology major because now I had decided that I wanted to skip nursing and go straight to studying to become a doctor. My curriculum consisted of a lot of science and math due to my field of study. For the most part, I held good grades and was doing well in class.

Halfway through my first semester, I began to go through problems at home. My mother had been diagnosed with lung cancer and had to begin chemotherapy. This realization rocked my reality and drove me spiraling out of control. I began to perform poorly whenever I actually attended class. The instructor noticed my obvious slip, but I couldn't overcome it. My ability to focus was off. This wasn't all because now I had begun to realize a factor that I hadn't before. This reality changed the course of my studies.

I would begin to attend the hospital visits with my mother and watch some of the procedures she would have to go through. I was very healthy, and I rarely had to go to the hospital for anything other than a check-up. So I hadn't even realized that I really couldn't stand the sight of blood. This was a idea that hadn't occurred to me before, and this blew my mind on the fact that I knew in my heart that I didn't want to be in the health field. I had run into another dead end, a costly mistake of judgement.

Understand, I am in no part justifying going to college

without a plan. In doing so you set yourself up for a very expensive failure. You should never attend college because you feel as if it's the next logical choice or you don't know what else to do. College is one of the most expensive options that you will encounter because they aren't just schools but they are classified as big businesses. So don't get that misunderstood.

There are countless former students and graduates who suffer from a ton of school debt. This debt stems from student loans and financial aid due to the high tuition fees to attend a college, the expensive books, and even more expensive housing. There are ways to apply for scholarships and to receive grant money. The good thing about these two is that you are required to pay the funds back. Use all resources that are made available to you.

If you decide that gaining a college degree is the correct path for you then let's talk. It's time to strategize a plan of attack. You never want to jump into any situation without proper planning. The key is to always look at the situation from the perspective of the bigger picture. You always want to have the endgame in mind by planning from the end to how you will actually get there.

Be sure to understand exactly what you want to accomplish once you complete your program. If you want to become a lawyer then you need to know the curriculum plan to become a lawyer. You want the plan for any issues that may be presented along the way. You want a straight laced laid out plan here. If you're not able or don't want to plan this alone then enlist the assistance of the counselors at the school that you plan to attend. These counselors will sit down to plan your educational path with you because it is their job to do so. I recommend meeting with these counselors even if you do think you know what you're doing because it can really help.

The field that you have selected is to become your career, your livelihood, so treat it as such. If you have chosen your field correctly then this process will not be hard for you because you will enjoy the challenge. Do not waste your time by allowing it to be stolen away from you through wasted decisions. Take your studies serious and this path will run smoothly for you and take you to where you need and want to be.

Let's begin with choosing the right college for you. This decision is more complicated than one would think. It depends on your field of choice and your personality. There are some colleges that have better programs for certain fields and they usually have a higher graduation rate. These colleges are a target for employers who are looking for employers who graduate from these schools due to the efficiency of the program.

You must also be careful to choose a college that is tailored to your personality. If you are not interested in attending big campuses and being a part of the whole university feel, then opt for a smaller school like a community college first. I recommend the community college route to anyone who hasn't been in school for a while and if they need to get back in the feel of things. Going to a community college first can be a great choice.

If you choose to attend community college first to gain your associate degree then you are one up on anybody who chose the alternate route. By attending a CC first, you get to work yourself back in rhythm by attending the classes that are more student focused. The instructions here are usually more inclined to teach their students hands-on rather than to just dictate a lesson to you. This is also a cheaper tuition alternative when compared to a full university.

CC's costs much less than a university therefore it's best to take any prerequisites here first. Prerequisites are sort of like the electives of your college curriculum. They are the classes that are not necessarily focused on your field but are required to earn your degree. It's best to take as many of these pre reqs in cc where classes cost less.

The great thing is that once you graduate and decide to transfer to a university that all of your school credits from the cc will transfer. This means you will not have to take the same class twice. Another plus is that you can use your Associate's degree while attending the university. You can work a job in your field on a lower level with this degree, while earning your bachelor's degree. This will help you with much-needed experience and money.

Once you've decided on the school that is right for you then it's time to gather up some financial aid. There are two types of financial aid for school and it's simple -- the kind you have to pay and the kind you don't have to pay back. Unless you have the money to pay for it yourself you'll have to apply for some form of financial aid. Let's discuss some of the financial aid options now.

Let's begin with scholarships and grants --- the financial aid that you don't have to pay back. Scholarship offers are usually based off your ACT scores -- if you scored high enough on the exam then funds will be allotted to you in the form of financial aid. If this option isn't the applicable for you then there are countless other scholarship foundations that come from different organizations. All it takes is a google search to find them and apply.

These scholarships usually have different requirements in order to qualify. Some of them may focus on helping students that are fresh out of high school, your local bank may have scholarships funds available if you kept a certain GPA, and there are some scholarship funds that require you to volunteer some of your spare time for worth causes in order to qualify.

Grants are also an option for financial aid that isn't expected to be paid back. These grants usually come from different parts of government and nonprofit organizations. Each grant usually focuses on a specific group of people. You may find one that is specially made for recently released inmates. There are some that focus on urban youth or people with disabilities. There are various grant specifications, and these are only a few examples so find those that relate to you.

Don't ever be too proud to ask for help because closed mouths don't get fed. Besides these nonprofits and businesses gain tax breaks by donating these funds to students in need. Some non-profits are created just to create tuition funds for financially challenged students. Think of it like this, -- whether you apply or not the money will be donated to someone regardless. The funds might as well be issued to you.

Now it's time to discuss federal financial aid and student

loans. For the most part, financial aid isn't required to pay back. You will apply for these funds by visiting the federal financial aid website. You will go through an application process that will basically be a summary of personal information and financial information that will determine your eligibility. Once you complete the basics you are prompted to send your financial aid award to the schools.

You will have the option of sending your financial aid to up to a certain number of schools. Although you may already have the school in mind that you want to attend it is best to send it to alternatives as well. You want to always give yourself an abundance of options when planning any of these financial inquiries. Once the school receives the inquiry the school will begin to send you the preparations to apply.

After completing the FAFSA applications you will almost instantly be given an award letter confirming how much financial aid that you are eligible for. Sometimes these funds are not enough to cover the full tuition and supplies but there are other options. Usually, there are state financial aid funds in which you can apply online. The final page of the financial aid application usually presents a link to apply for these funds.

If needed, student loans are a costly option since these funds are required to be paid back. You can usually apply for these directly through the school's website. These funds don't come cheap because they are combined with interest fees to be paid back usually through a payment plan of the same sorts. The thing about student loans is that the payments are not due until after you've finished your education. Meaning that you are not obligated to pay until you graduate or have defaulted on the payments by not returning to school after a period of time. Failure to pay these funds back can result in a multitude of financial debt and wage garnishments.

If you default on a payment for your student loans this will result in a negative infraction on your credit report. These defaulted payments are one of the few negative marks that cannot be removed off your credit unless paid. These payments can then be subject to garnishment. This can be accomplishd in the form of being taken out of your annual income tax refund. They could even go as far as garnishing a portion of your employment paycheck. That's tough huh? So be careful with your money and don't waste your time and credit.

Since this is such a big mark on your financial history you plan accordingly. After every quarter of a semester if there is money that is still left over after paying your tuition and supplies the remainder will be given to you in the form of a student refund. Every year young adults are paid these student refunds and they buy things that they need such as a car, they pay bills, buy furniture, housing, etc. This is understanding because these are good things to buy with the money but once you've acquired the necessities you can now do better with the remaining funds.

You can in turn take your refund and begin to use it to pay on some of the school debt prematurely. This will give you a head start on the payments in order to give you the advantage. If you are a business or investment-minded person you could save this money to the side for the purpose using it for seed money. This is a good idea for the loan because the business or investment will begin to pay the loan off over time by itself, or you could simply just save the money until you have developed the right plan for it. Either choice is better than just spending the money recklessly.

Surprisingly - a lot of people take this money for immature reasons. I remember a time when people would attend college just to receive the refund. The problem is that once they received the refund, they would abruptly stop attending school. This would in turn create an extremely negative mark on their credit report and on their educational report if they did choose to return. An incomplete in more ways is worse on a report than the flaw of a failing grade. Remember it's not worth the debt you will receive. If you choose to attend for the money then at least attend for something you know you'll complete while making it worth while.

For the convicted brothers and sisters that are reading this part, please don't be intimidated. The only crime that usually prevents you from recieving federal financial aid is drug charges.

Even if you have drug charges, there are alternate forms of financing available for the recently released felons. Most colleges are felon friendly and even if you're not comfortable attending the campus you can attend online classes instead.

With online classes you will be able to dictate the way that you may attend class better. This is a better fit for someone who has a larger commute than most, or a person who isn't comfortable in a classroom setting. You will be able to customize your classes to fit in with your schedule in order to be able to attend class at your best. With the way that the world is headed this may be the future of all classrooms indeed.

Remember: Earning a college degree is an important step in life and graduation college demands respect. So once you decide on an educational path please take these classes seriously and try your best to perform. I want you to understand that college isn't for everyone and for this particular set of readers let's move on to the next chapter to discuss some other options.

CHAPTER 8

Trade/Internship

    We have previously discussed some of the information regarding trades and/or vocational training. To learn a trade is to learn a lifelong skill in order to make money to provide for yourself/your family. For most people gaining a trade is more important than earning a college degree and I can understand their plight. A trade usually takes 2 years to learn and you can begin to work using the trade almost instantaneously after you have earned it. Some college students go years without employment in their field post graduation; mostly because they have chosen the wrong field. Another reason is that gaining a trade is more of a hands-on physical education compared to the college's book-taught, read-only learning. These two comparisons alone can make gaining a trade seem to be more desirable.

    I know a guy from the neighborhood that I am from who wasn't that blessed in book smarts. He went through grade school apart of the special education program. Some people mistake specialized classes for "Slow" people but in actuality, these are regular students who have different learning disabilities that cause them to learn uniquely. This did not stop him from becoming a successful business owner. He now owns 2 tattoo parlors and 3 car washes and his businesses are constantly scaling. He will even tell you that people thought he was dumb but what he knows is how to conduct business.

    Jeff Bezos, the world's richest man, did attend college, and it was one of the highest-rated colleges in America. He was extremely intelligent as well; I mean he had to be to get accepted to Princeton University. Although he was very intelligent, he still chose to drop out of college in order to go another route. He chose to start a business that will revolutionize the shopping world. You can see where this decision had led him.

Needless to say -- college isn't the only formal education available. I realized this in the spring of 2013 when I finally began to discover my true path. Initially, I chose to go to JSU on my scholarship but slowly began to lose interest due to my family problems. This is the point I realized that I had chosen the wrong field and that medicine wasn't the right path for me. So I ended up taking a break from college.

Years went by as I went without a formal education. I would work as a skilled labor for my uncle's brick masonry company. The work was hard and straining labor. We would have to work through the extreme weather conditions of Mississippi. It was nothing for the temperure to reach 105° in the summertime and the heat would blanket around you like a glove. I was wasting my brain away by not feeding it the knowledge that I knew it craved. Until the day I decided that it was time to go back to school.

True enough while working with my uncle I was learning a trade through hands on experience and apprenticeship. I knew that this was something that would take a lot of my time to learn due to the process in which my uncle was teaching me to lay bricks. I knew that this wasn't exactly what I wanted to do with my life, but I knew it could play a part in my financial success. Then I had an epiphany.

When I was growing up I was gifted with computers. I received my first computer when I was 14 years old and I fell in love with it. My first computer was a Gateway hot wheels computer with the Windows operating system. I had begun experiment with music production and I began to produce hip-hop instrumentals to record my friends and my songs over. I would use fruity loops and pro tools to perfom these tasks..

My computer wasn't equipped to support the newmusic software, so I had to find a better way. My mother owned a gateway desktop as well but hers was more advanced than mine. One day we wanted to record a new track so I decided to install the software on my mother's computer instead. Everything was going fine until the software caused my mother's computer to crash.

I panicked because my mother had strictly asked me not to mess with her computer because I had my own. I had to do something quickly so I decided to replace her hard drive with mine. I had been taking the time to explore the inside of the CPU and felt quite comfortable with the disassembly. It was a success and just in time before she got home off work.

When she got home she went through her normal routine and then she sat on her computer ready to play her games online. I knew the hardware install had been successful, but I didn't account for one thing. She immediately noticed that something was wrong when she boot up the computer and all of my programs began to load up. I didn't think of the fact that my computer's interface would show up on her device. She was mad and oh boy she was hot, but she was also impressed.

She was surprised that I knew as much as I did about the makeup of the computer and being able to repair it. As time went on, she became so confident in my skills that she began to advertise my skills as services at her job. I had begun to fix her co-workers computers and would get paid a nice sum of money. I hadn't realized that this could be my calling before. I decided that this is what I should go to school for. So, I decided to attend the local community college for computer service technology in order to earn my Associate Degree in Applied Science. This is an important point in my life because I found a cause worth learning for. This is what I want you to take the time to seek out.

Inside each of us, there is a gift that is hungry with a strong need for training. It is our destiny to find this gift and feed it the necessary knowledge so that it may grow into the skill that we need it to be. This skill in turn, will become a tool for use in your career path to financial success. Once you find this gift you should strategize a plan around this gift and begin with earning your certifications.

Remember- the degree shouldn't be your only focus. While in the process of gaining your degree seek to earn as many certificates that you can in your field. What some students fail to realize is that the certifications earn you the good positions and get you the pay raises. Every field of study has certifications that you can earn such as OSHAA safety, forklift, machinery operation, etc.

During the education phase of your life, one of the most important things to remember is to network. You should constantly network with other students that practice in or in relation to your field of study. These people are the next generation of leaders in this career and its best to know them now. You never know when you could use their expertise on a project or their reference on a job. I can't say this enough, take this education serious!

CHAPTER 8

Conclusion (Read)

I must conclude this chapter with another antidote of my experience but it's the most important one of them all. The year was 2014 and I was attending college, earning my associate degree in computer science technology. At the time I was fixing computers in my spare time charging a decent fee and making an reasonable income. For a college student, I was doing rather well. One day I was lounging in my downtime with a group of friends. 2 male associates, their girlfriends and my girlfriend.

We were playing some music and chilling together. When my next-door neighbor came over and invaded our gathering. He began to brag about how he's been running my uncle's brick masonry business because my uncle was tending to personal issues. He kept boasting of making $18 per hour and how much money he was saving. To us, it seemed as if he came over to simply brag in front of us and our woman.

I saw the looks that were on my friend's faces, which was a look of puzzlement and intrusion. I had an epiphany that changed the way that I looked at life from that point on. So I decided to confront the situation. At this point, I was a small-time entrepreneur and hustler. I would burn 100's of CDs and DVDs and sell them wholesale to my friend Twan. Twan would in turn sell the CDs for 3 for $10.00 and DVDs 2 for $10.00. I was also repairing computers and phones for students at school and events that I had ran across. After analying these facts through my head I had thought of a point of attack.

After polling Twan about his cd and dvd operation, I concluded that on the average day everyone in the room earned more money per hour than my neighbor. Twan managed to persuede most of the customers to purchase at least 2-3 discs each visit. With that said he averaged a decent pay of upwards to $60 an hour. He pays me $1.50 a disc in which pays back my initial investments with a profit.

I fixed computers on the side and attended school on my side time. I had a decent amount of clientele. The cheapest service that I provided was a virus clean in which I charged $59.99. This virus clean usually took me 2 hours to complete. This allowed for me to at least earn $30.00 per hour on a regular basis. Even my friend Marcus who worked two minimum wage jobs managed to make more than him considering these factors.

This sudden realization of information seemed to embarrass my neighbor as he turned to escape. We all got a huge laugh off his reaction but I continued to think of this for days. This is when I realized that we as humans are constantly at odds with the nature of time. It's a losing battle to say the least because in the end, time will always reigns supreme. Time doesn't have to be our enemy at all, it can also be our ally while we live in this world.

Instead of fighting against time, we can make time work for us. This led me to think of my uncle as a boss. As a labor I would be paid $10.00 per hour but it seemed that no matter how hard I worked or the type of job that we worked I always was paid in the same pay range. This is when I realized that my uncle used the clock against us. He promoted hard work and higher rates of production in order to get as much work done in a small amount of time. Once he accomplished this to a certain degree, he would begin to manipulate the work clock.

See, my uncle already knew how much money he wanted to make for himself. Therefore he knows how much he had to pay us in order to account for this pay for himself. In order to accomplish this, all he did was control the amount of hours that we worked a day. By doing this no matter how hard we worked we would only earnwhat he wanted to pay us. I called this pimping the clock my friend.

After realizing this, I decided that my time was worth more to me than $10.00 an hour and I set out to pimp the clock for myself. We all are given the same basics, the same 24 hours a day but it is your decision to choose what you do with your time. Rap artist, producer, and entrepreneur Sean "P Diddy" Combs is quoted to have said that he only sleeps a maximum of 3 hours a day. Now I am not asking you not to rest because to do so can be quite counterproductive. What I am saying to you is to make your time count for something productive.

As we get older the more time seems to pass us over quicker and this can mean a great amount of wasted time for us if we are unproductive. I can write this book and tell you an almost guaranteed strategy to become a millionaire but if you are not using your time wisely then it will be in vain. I need you to do more than just read this but to implement this within your life and into your soul.

Success takes more than talent or intelligence. True success takes motivation and ambition. You must be able to look pass the have's and have not's in order to be able to see the bigger picture. Where do you want to be 30 years from now? Do you want to be barely making it or do you want to be well off? If you want to be financially successful you have to begin now my friend.

Take control of your destiny by taking control of your time instead of watching that reality show tonight, let's study. Pick a time frame in your day to direct your focus towards productivity. Boost the value of your time by fitting more positive activities into your day. All this will work for your better good and pay off in dividends. Practice repetition and learn to take the time to read on your own. Don't allow time to conquer you, you have to learn to pimp the clock, Now let's discuss one of the most important methods in order to do so...

Section 3

Chapter 9 - Business (Intro)

In order to truly take back control of your time, you must practice the strategy of minding your own business. The city that I am from is a city similar to yours. There is an extreme shortage of jobs and an almost non existant amount of resources and money. The jobs that are available are almost impossible to get hired on at because the staff will usually hire their family and friends. Even if you do pass the background checks and drug tests you will still have to know somebody who knows somebody in order to get hired. If hired the pay is so small that there is no way possible for you to make a honest living.

These jobs usually are dead end with not much hope for advancement. Due to the lack of skills that this job requires it leaves no room for the future. So, most of our brothers and sisters turn to other forms of making money in order to make up for the lack of resources. We turn to drugs and alcohol for an escape from this harsh reality that plagues us through our boredom and fears. The only way to break this cycle is through true motivation and ambition.

You must turn this ambition into a sense of urgency to own your future. To accomplish this you must own your own work and realize your free creativity. The times of our grandparents are over with. Back when they were able to attend school to make good grades and get a good caree. In their day this was the ultimate plan because it was the responsibility of the employer to provide retirement for their employees. These days when our parents, aunts and uncles retire some barely have enough retirement funds distributed monthly to be able to take care of themselves. How will you compensate for this?

Don't ever become dependent upon a paycheck in order to care for your family and yourself. The bible says that if you depend on a man that you'll forever be let down. What will happen if the company you've worked for faithfully each day files bankruptcy and they have to conduct a major lay off? You will have to fend for yourself with whatever you have left if you were even able to save money. Don't blame the CEO for your problem, you must blame yourself. For its human nature to act in self-perservance and you should as well.

   Through business ownership, you gain more responsibility in your life. Through this venture, you begin to make time work for you. This is the true beauty of life. This is the only true path to wealth and financial success. So find a field that you relate to and study each aspect of it. For a path that you are fond of will create a more enjoyable and meaningful process. Then let's begin.

CHAPTER 9

Business:

I remember the years after recently being released from jail. I was young, black, and I had a felony on my record. These were the strikes against me outside of my neighborhood and when I did venture outside I was constantly reminded of my transgressions immediately. What I didn't lack was ambition and a great amount of charisma which I would use to my advantage.

I knew I couldn't allow myself to dwell on my flaws but I had to use my abilities to progress. I only knew two ways to make money at this point: the illegal way and the legal way and I was fed up with illegal procedures. The legal path that I knew was to get a 9 to 5 job and/or go to school. School was questionable at this point due to defaulted student financial aid payments, so a job was my only option.

Up to this point I had worked for my uncle's brick masonry company as a laborer but the conditions were harsh. The work was hard labor in which I would work through the hottest summers, even through the coldest winters that were allowed. I felt like it was taking my uncle too long to teach me how to lay bricks so I was beginning to see no future in this trade. Believe me, I was no stranger to hard work, but I often longed for a better job.

So, I decided to go on a focused job search where I applied to every job that I felt I was qualified for including grocery stores, Walmart, family dollar, clothing stores and even McDonalds and other fast-food restaurants. Boy, was this a disheartening process for me. I slowly began to realize the truth of reality and the outlook was dim. That is was in my city, and I wasn't employable in my own hometown.

This indeed was a result of the 3 negatives factors that I stated earlier but there were other factors that were working against me as well. There was an extreme job shortage in my city due to the counterproductive concepts such as high crime rate, lack of resources, and no interest in building or growth in the area. Big companies didn't see the point of bringing their business to our city. This combined with the dangerous environment we had to endure was the cause for employment oppression. The few jobs that were available were employed upon a who is who basis which made the situation worse. I quickly concluded that this will be a lost cause.

So how would I provide for myself? How could I progress to the path of accomplishing my goals? I was stunned by reality and continued to work for my uncle until 1 day I saw the light. I began to look around my neighborhood and noticed that everyone wasn't hustling for illegal money. I saw some people with lawn movers, and weed eaters strapped onto trailers of their trucks. I thought of my uncles and their business and I knew what had to be done. I had to start my own business but how and what kind?

Business ideas

In order to start a business, you must first decide what type of business that you're interested in. There are some key issues to debate before you start. You must first conduct an assessment of yourself. What is it that drives you? What is it that you are passionate about? Of course, you must have some type of skill or gift in this field as well, but the know-how can be taught and learned hands-on. Begin to take an inventory of any field of business that you think you will be successful within.

Now take into consideration the supply and demand. Every successful business supplies a much-needed service. In order to do this, pay attention to your environment and take account of any needs. After you begin to take account of the needs -- begin to think of ways to fill this void. This is the way of business and this is the way to success. Don't ever begin a business without first establishing a demand.

Third, always start any venture with an ending in mind. You must always keep your mind open to see the bigger picture. A business owner should have an idea of what he wants to accomplish before he even begins. This will keep your inspiration in tune and your motivation high. Please remember never to allow your excitement for the outcome to cause you to be impatient. Always pay attention to detail for this is the key to a successful business.

Once you have chosen a business field it is time to put on your bookbag and put your face in some books. To be successful in a business you must learn as much about the field as possible. You can do this through going to a vocational college and/or on your own through reading books on the topic. Please take detailed notes as you learn in order to refer back to as you are going through your hands-on learning. I cannot express this enough -- reading is very necessary and without it, you will have a very difficult path laid ahead for you and can result in failure.

Interlude

It was spring of 2015 and I was attending college. I had begun to perfom additional jobs at school; fixing students' computers and phones. I had even started to do furniture moving jobs, subcontracting for my own brick masonry team and running a landscape business. I felt I was doing good with myself and was becoming mildly successful in my efforts. I was known as the computer head, the college student and I began to become popular in my neighborhood.

One day I ran across a fellow neighborhood entrepreneur at the corner store while grabbing some snacks. We usually exchanged handshakes when we ran across each other's paths and we would engage in decent conversation. I knew him as the guy who was buying up the houses in the hood and renovating them. I was impressed with his work and wanted to learn the process. I pulled him to the side to ask him how could I get into real estate. He gave me an answer I wasn't prepared for.

He was actually kind of happy I asked. He told me that he had heard that I was rather intelligent and that I was among the few small business owners on this side of town. He thought that real estate would be a great fit for me. So he walked off and wrote something down and handed it to me. On the paper it was the name of a book and he told me to read it, then call him. Needless to say, I was disappointed.

I had felt like t he was letting me down easy and was throwing me a curve ball. I couldn't believe this guy was asking me to read a book. Especially when he could just teach me himself. I threw the paper away in disgust and vowed to make it on my own by any means. Little did I know that the guy was actually pointing me in the right direction.

Business Plans:

After you have researched and have selected a category for entrepreneurship it is time to sit down to form a strategy. First, you must choose the type of business entity that is best for you. There are a few such as; limited liability, limited partnerships, sole proprietorship, etc. Each one of these will have their own distinct characteristics and qualities that make them unique for different businesses. The best entity for a small business is LLC's and sole proprietorships due to the levels of security and ownership.

The sole proprietorship is a more adapted for self-employed businessmen. This is due to the fact that the business owner will be the sole owner of this business. This also means that all responsibility falls on the owner and this can be costly. There is no degree of protection for the owner from the legal issues of the company. This means you are the company and if you are sued everything you own becomes attainable through litigation.

Limited liability corporations or LLC', are the most popular of the entities. A lot of this stems from the fact that as the owner of an LLC you are granted the greatest amount of protection available through this entity. This means if your company comes under legal attack that you are not a personally being attacked. Therefore, if you are to lose in court proceedings the only property and/or resources at risk are that of the company, your personal life and possessions are safe. This entity also allows for the best potential for tax breaks. So, sit down and do some research on the entity you want to choose because the decision can be vital.

There are a few ways to file these entities in order to make them legitimate. One way is to fill out and send in the paperwork yourself. You do this by either buying the packet online or at your local Office Depot. Once you fill this out and file it then you're mostly complete. This is the best way to save money becauseit will only cost you $50.00 to $100.00. The other way is to contact a lawyer to file the packet for you but this can cost anywhere between $300.00 to $500.00. It's your choice.

Next you must file your business with the state that you

will operate in and you can do this online. This will cost you no more than $25.00 depending on the state you apply in, completing this will grant you your tax id number and federal Ein number. The tax id number is used in compliance if you are to be selling products to customers and will be used to file taxes annually. The Federal Ein is the businesses' social security number, but we will discuss this later in detail.

Once you've completed these processes it's time to form a strategy. This strategy will be materialized in the form of a business plan. A business plan is a very detailed breakdown of your business and what you project to accomplish through the timeline of your venture. The more detailed the better. This plan is one of the most important parts of your business because it will be referred to through the majority of your business' life. We're going to discuss some of the important factors surrounding a business plan during the initial setup.

The business plan is designed in order to give you guidance. The act of brainstorming and planning alone will direct you to which direction to commit to next in your business venture. It also serves as sort of reference in order to know where you're headed next. The plan is basically a map that is best used to navigate through your goal path. So for this reason alone you want to be as detailed as possible. You will want to take the time to plan up to 20 years and more from the day of creation. Plan big and you will be sure to hit your mark.

Your business plan is also the tool needed to establish funding. If you're not financially strong enough to provide a sufficient initial investment, then fundraising is the next best option available. In order to successfully win over lenders and investors you will need the services of a professionally prepared business plan. The two most important issues that lenders will pay attention to when declaring wheither to lend money is the business structure and pricing factors.

The business structure will express to the reader the true concept of the business and what you are providing to the world. This will give the lender a glimpse into what will make the business tick but more important who will make it tick. A lender will want to know the who is who of the business. They want to know the chain of power organization of the business. This is important to them because in the event that you may not be able to run the company, or something happens to you then someone will need to run the company to pay their money back.

Yes, it should be no surprise, the most important point for the lender is their return on investment (R.O.I.). They want to know how and when their money is going to get paid back with interest. So the business is meant to provide all this information within a professional presentation. You should be sure to express in clear detail all the services rendered and fees you're planning to charge. Be sure to list any marketing strategies that you plan to initiate in order generate money at high rates.

If you're putting together your business plan on your own then there are some efficient ways of accomplishing this. You could start by performing a google search for a sample business plan. You could even find a sample business plan based on your type of business. This sample business plan is meant to give you an outline or a model for you to model your business plan after. You will then insert your own original ideas and projections.

The other option is to find a professional in order to aid you in the plan creation. This option will cost you some money, but it would be well spent, or you could visit your local SBA office and obtain assistance for free. Whatever method that you choose please be sure to take your time and focus on this plan. I can't stress the importance of this plan enough. The presence of a good business plan could either make or break a business, through funding or lack of efficient planning.

Interlude:

In 2017 I was convicted and sentenced into a federal penitentiary for 18 months. This was my first time ever being sentenced to prison time. I wanted this be my last as well. In order to accomplish this, I knew I had to stay focused on something productive and mind my own business. So I decided early on that I would not allow my time to be wasted. They had me incarcerated physically but my mind will stay free.

I suggest this to all my readers who are currently incarcerated. Although you are cage up physically, you can still own your time. You do this by making productive use of your time by staying positive and persistent. This time can become whatever you decide it will be for you – this sentence can be a college for you or a training process. This doesn't have to be a waste of your life. Especially if you are released with more knowledge than you had when you came in.

This was exactly my mind state when I got to the federal facility. I began to read books on everything productive that I was interested in. My studies involved everything from real estate, stock market, investing, to different types of business. What was helpful was that it was great multitude of inmates that were experienced in these subjects. Some even were willing to sit down with me to discuss in depth what makes up these concepts. There were even classes that were dedicated to some of these subjects.

Matter of fact; the first month that I was there a real estate class was about to begin and of course I signed up. This class was being taught by a former real estate investor from the east coast that was very experienced in the subject. The class was packed. The first day of class he started with a bunch of basics to warm up the class.

The second day I noticed the class attendance was smaller with at least half of the audience that attended the first day missing. I didn't take much of it because I was deeply focused on the lesson at hand. This class was full of "game". He taught us multiple strategies and broke down the more detailed approaches. I was in a state of educational bliss.

The third and final class held no more than 7 of us. It was a great recap of the class with a few added ideas. I was impressed. At the end of the class we were given our makeshift certificates of completion and began to exit. I was so happy with the amount of knowledge that I had received that I ran to catch up with the teacher to shake his hand. When I did reach him I immediately express my gratitude by telling him thank you in which he asked "Why?". After recalling the guy at the store, I then told him, "Because you just blessed me with a million dollars' worth of game and you don't even know me."

Business accounts/funding:

After completing the process of incorporating your business it's time to begin the financial side of this process. There are many ways to raise funds, but the first step of this process is through starting a business bank account. This is also an important step into beginning to build your business credit as well.

In order to begin the process, you must visit the guy responsible for the business accounts at your banks. By now you should have a pretty good relationship with the bank due to your personal accounts being there. The best bank to start these accounts with are the bigger banks that are nationwide. Due to their size and experience with handling businesses' money they will be more reasonable with funding.

Since you've completed the last process you now have the preparation needed to start this account. Equipped with your EIN and incorporation paperwork visit the bank business office in order to meet with the agent. Once you've set up this account you will begin to notice that you'll begin to receive business credit applications, business loans and business discounts. This is due to a very important cause.

When I first began to receive these offers, I didn't know why, and it wasn't until years later when I studied on the financial responsibility of incorporating a business that it began to understand. It's previously stated the Ein is considered to be the business's social security number so as with a social you must protect it due to the extreme importance of this number.

With this Ein number comes a completely separate line of credit. This means that you can build it up through the same methods that you used with your personal credit. The difference is that this credit is on another level. You begin the same way by starting to flow cash in and out of the account. Mostly you want use checks, direct transfers, etc. for the paper trail. This will help when wanting to apply for a loan and later when you need to file business taxes.

Once you begin to build a business relationship with the

bank you'll be able to apply for credit. The easiest way is to begin applying is through the business credit cards, and store business cards. Once you get approved you will receive a much bigger spending limit than you are used to. This doesn't mean that you should splurge on unnecessary items. Instead you should use this credit to invest into your business and pay back the credit either early or on time. This will build your business credit.

To apply successfully for a business loan will require you to display a more detailed and professional presentation than you created for the simple credit application. This is when your business plan and your personal reputation are going to come into use. The initial route of funding is usually triggered by applying for credit through your business's bank.

At your bank you will schedule a meeting with the business loan officer. You should take this meeting very seriously and approach the meeting professionally. Dress in business attire and be careful to arrive for the meeting at least 15 minutes early. Be sure to have your business plan professionally combed through and practice your pitch beforehand. It is always a good idea to dress your business plan in a professional, yet classy folder.

Within the meeting you must present yourself as charismatic and as business intelligent as possible. You want to smile and stick to the main subjects of your business structure and how you are planning to pay back the loan. Focus on your board of directors and your pricing and marketing strategies. Always be prepared to respond to any questions asked. You must be presentable with confidence because confidence is key.

If you were persuasive enough and your presentation was efficient you'll have an answer shortly. Usually the loan officer will look over the business plan, evaluate it and get back to you within days. Even if you've not initially approved, the bank will usually monitor your account for recorded cash flow and grant you a business line of credit.

This line of credit will be in the form of a decent sized overdraft option on your business' debit card. This is a wonderful opportunity to gain some of the financial funding needed and to build on your business credit history with the bank. The plan is to use this credit and any credit you receive to buy tools you need for the business, and pay back the funds promptly. If this isn't enough there are other ways to receive funding.

There are countless organizations that are dedicated to providing affordable loans to small businesses. One of such is an SBA loan. You will apply with a local branch of SBA and schedule a visit with a loan officer there. This process will be much similar to the meeting with the bank officer, so be sure to be prepared with a business plan in hand.

If you are a felon then there are some organizations that are operating to help you. There are also government assistance programs that are available for recently released inmates to be able to receive small business funds. All you need to do is follow the steps that I've previously listed and apply. Check the resources for some of these organizations.

You can also enlist the services of a hard money lender. These lenders are usually independent investors who are looking to make money off a good business venture. When dealing with these lenders you can expect higher than usual interest rates and an extensive conditions of payments. The good thing is that these lenders are usually more lenient when deciding to loan money. Be careful because these loans can become very expensive. Just remember these key things when you do receive proper funding.

Interlude

As my release date from the federal facility approached, I began to consult with more and more productive people. I had been established at the facility as sort of a brainiac because of my long hours I spent in the library studying. I was the winning horse that everyone was betting on to succeed and to never come back. This had earned me a invitation from the Muslims.

The leaders of the Muslim group had noticed my ambition and persistence. They had an upcoming event scheduled that was targeted at the younger inmates. It was meant to be a summit of speakers who would attempt to direct the youth away from violence and gang activity and towards legal financial endeavors. They offered me a position to speak at the summit.

I was surprised by the invitation and was extremely proud of their nomination. Although everybody at the facility knew that I wasn't a Muslim, I was obliged to accept. There was no way I could miss an opportunity to talk to a group of young brothers in a positive light. I always knew that I wanted help people in a productive way but there was a problem. What was I to talk about?

I was at a loss because during my time there. I have studied a multitude of subjects. How and what subjects to choose was the question. So I decided to consult with one of my associates who was sort of a mentor of mine. He explained to me that I could discuss anything I wanted because I had taken the time and patience to study these subjects. I had already worked and gained experience in the world by starting and operating my own businesses. Then it came to me.

What had aided me throughout my journey of knowledge and experience was my own ambition and dertimination. It was my inspiration and motivation that caused me to stay persistent in seeking knowledge. I willed myself to stay in the library studying for hours on end. This is what these young brothers should hear.

I came to the realization that I could give away all the knowledge that I had learned but it could still be in vain. If I were to tell you step by step how to earn a fortune but you lacked the ambition then there is no point. As the real estate class got smaller each class; people usually lack the will to accept and apply.

To truly learn a craft and to master it in order to apply it to your success you must work hard. This means you must execute long hours of study every day; you must be willing to sacrifice your fun for the present in order secure your success in the future. Without this kind of ambition: success is nearly impossible. For the bible tells you "Life is but a wind." You must live your life and make every minute meaningful. A focused path to your success.

In conclusion, there are some goals you are to be sure to accomplish once you're fully funded and operating. You must remember at all times to provide professionalism and to produce good business habits. A business's ethics will speak for itself. In order to continue to prosper and attract success you must work hard and never break the ethics code by any means. It is a known fact that quality business begets more clients.

To accomplish this you must be sure to have quality employees. Your employees are a representation of the establishment that you operate. I know that in this generation it is becoming harder and harder to find efficient employees but it's still some left. The key is hire by their qualities and characteristics. Take your time and assess your potential hire. One bad apple can truly spoil the bunch

Last but never least, reinvest. If you are planning grow a successful business venture that has the potential to scale, you must reinvest your profit to expand. This is the equivalent of betting on yourself. If you're a winner and have confidence in your model, then this is considered to be a sure bet.

Section 4:

Investing

This section is a very essential topic but also the most neglected. The art of investing is truly invaluable in the acquisition of wealth. A lot of people fail to understand the concepts that make up wealth. This causes them to shy away or even fear this path. Some get caught up in advertisements of flipping cash quick and try their hand at it only to fail miserably.

Investing is not to be feared but it is not to be underestimated either. This path can lead you to financial bliss and take you to levels that you could only fathom. The key to success in investing is in the due diligence. You have to sit down and will yourself to learn this enigma. The knowledge and experience aren't something that will come to you overnight but will begin to bless your brain tenfold if you choose to explore it.

There are a multitude of investment vehicles but there are only two major kinds of investing flows – long term and short term. It is through assessment of your financial makeup that you find which is best for you. Every investment vehicle that you come across has the ability to become either a financial disaster or a financial blessing.

A long-term vehicle is characterized by being low risk. This is because your money is usually invested over a lengthy period of time. This gives you more time to take your funds out of the vehicles faster if it is tanking. This flow is for the people who have decent sums of money sitting idle. Instead, you choose to park that money into a good long term vehicle to draw more interest from it. The problem is that this will take much longer to build profit than the alternative.

Short term vehicles are riskier due to the speed in which these vehicles fluctuate. Most of these investments incur positions that usually expire or pay off in days, weeks or within a few months. These vehicles call for more knowledge but grant extremely larger returns on investment. The bigger the risk the bigger the reward. A person can have a smaller amount of initial investment and triple their money in weeks. The problem here is that you are subject to lose more money in a shorter time. With these vehicles you have to be careful and take youre time to study.

CD's and Bonds.

The first form of investing that people are introduced to are through the banks. Banks are the kings of long term vehicles because they are the most reliable and well known. They also issue out the returns on investment through a tool called interest. Banks are in the business of keeping their account holders money safe and available to them at any time. They also are interested in other things as well.

A bank makes it money through a majority of ways - account fees, card fees, overdraft fees, etc. A bank's most profitable venture is through investing your money. Banks are the financial backers that power tons of businesses and investment ventures. They loan this money at a fee of interest. Since they've used your money to invest, they'll pay you a small form of interest over time. Well only if you have an interest drawing savings account. Isn't this convenient?

You are able to secure your money and make money off it all at once. The thing is that it'll take you decades to build any significant ROI off a savings account alone due to the small payouts. The bank's use this method in order to persuade you from taking your money out. It's starting to make sense huh? Regardless of the facts, there are more profitable vehicles within the bank as well.

Certified deposits (CD's) yield the higher interest rates on your money. These options usually double your ROI. First you must speak with the officer that is over this branch to inquire about buying a CD. You can buy these for various prices such as $200, $500, $1000 and on up. Once purchased you will sign a contract of length. This contract will explain that your money is to be kept in this vehicle for a specific length of time. If you follow through completely with the process then your ROI is usually doubled. If you cannot hold to the terms and prematurity withdraw then you will only receive a percentage of interest. The amount of interest fluctuates through different establishments.

Through all of this information that I've just described to you regarding banks I do not want to confuse you. Although banks are cheaper investing pay masters, they are the safest place to hold your money. A bank is always more secure than any other form that competes. Those prepaid debit cards do not usually come with any beneficial features. If you are going to park your money then you might as well make same money off of it while it sits.

Mutual Funds:

If you are looking to park your money in a vehicle with a high profit yield then mutual funds may be the right car for you. These vehicles are made for novice investors who have yet to fully study how to invest for themselves. This car will allow you to park any money that you have to spare to invest through a longer term of investing. The good thing about these funds are they are generally successful, less risk and earn the investor a bigger return.

Most mutual funds are run by groups of experienced and talented investors. These funds are made up of a multitude of clients and certified investors who invest the sum of the money into different ventures that they have picked as successful. These ventures can vary over a range of a variety of fields - stocks, businesses, project funding, real estate, etc.

Once the investors have completed a successful profit yield then its time to pay out. They will then calculate and pay profitable percentages to each investor. Your percentage value will depend on the amount of money that you initially invested and of course these savvy investors will charge a hefty commission but believe me that if they're successful in their endeavors then it is well deserved. There is a very small chance that you may lose some or all off your money in this deal.

The key to success with a mutual fund is through enlisting the services of skilled investors. To be able to analyze these investors you must know a little about the basics. You do this by reading a few books on the subject. Although this won't teach you everything that you need to know, it will help you to determine if mutual funds will be profitable for you.

Be sure to inquire about any and all ventures that the fund is invested in. Do some homework on some of these ventures on your own to determine their profitability. Most mutual funds offer different investment packages that are customed to the clients. They do this by analyzing your financial capabilities and then deciding on the level of your package-low, moderate and/or progressive.

Stock market

I know at some point we all have heard stories of the stock market and the large amounts of currency that it entails. There is a huge amount of money to be made but you can also lose a lot of it as well. Stock market investing is a long term vehicle that brings profit without much risk.

I know that you have heard of the stock market crashes that have devastated the economy. These disasters happened due to different conditions that caused these failures but it's still one fact that remains. You can build a good future from successful stock market investments. These stocks are representations of different businesses; commodities such as oil, aluminum, etc. and different currencies. Each of these stocks are evaluated daily for their worth and their value will fluctuate. It is through the knowledge of these stocks and trend following that you will make money.

Good knowledge of stock market investing will take a lot more studying than I could express in this book but I'll give you a glimpse within the basics to help you establish a will to learn. For example, there is a stock named Nvidia that has the potential to take the technology world by storm. If you take the time to do the due diligence on Nvidia and analyze their business structure and it reveals an upcoming promising project that may draw a great income, then you're in luck.

With this knowledge you have a potential money-making investment. You must determine the amount of time that you will need in order to grow your money. The average stock market investment can take 6 months to year or more to appreciate in value. So the money that you plan to invest should be money that you will not need immediately and that you can afford to lose. Never invest money that you can't afford to lose.

Once you decide on the amount of initial investment then it's time to purchase some stock. In order to do this you must either have your own brokerage account or acquire the help of an investor with a broker to do the trading. Setting up a brokerage account is rather easy. You'll have to fill out an application with the broker that will verify your identity, financial status and your general knowledge. Once accepted you must download the proper software to your phone and/or laptop, and fund your account to pay the stock.

Reminder that after you buy into the stock that the investing has just began. By being a stock owner, you now own a piece of the business that is determined by how much stock you hold. Due to this ownership you will begin to get quarterly payments that are called dividends. These dividends are on percentage of profits from the businesses quarterly report that are paid to the investors. That's not all through.

You must be able to follow your stocks on your own. You can do this through a multitude of ways-your software, news, online, etc. If the stock's value is trending up, then you continue buy or keep your position of up trending. This trend can change after a while so you have to pay attention to be able to catch the reversal in time. If you catch wind of a loss in the upcoming report or some type of bad news then you have other options to consider. You could sell your stocks at a profit and move on, or you can keep your position and stay for the ride if you expect the trend to return to the uptrend. The choice is yours to make.

If you lack confidence in your own knowledge there's other options. You could acquire a skilled investor that can invest your money for you. First be sure that this investor is legit by cross checking their credentials and references. If all is well then you will be assessed financially and assigned a portfolio. The investor then will begin to handle the buying and selling of your stocks in a profitable manner. With that said there will be a commission fee that the broker will charge but if they're efficient then it's worth the charge.

Day trading is another form of stock trading that is much riskier but offers a much larger profit yield. The two most popular day trading forms are future and options. These forms of trading are slightly similar to the regular stock market but the actual trading is extremely volatile. Day trading consists of entering the market in the beginning of the day and exiting in a short time range – anywhere from exiting that day to a few days later. This form of investing is too risky to invest large sums of money and jump in without any knowledge. I suggest only initiating trades if you have taken the time to gain the knowledge and experience needed. You have been warned.

Real estate

It's only right that after discussing stock market trading that I discuss their arch nemesis, real estate investors. I never knew that these guys were sort of in competition with each other until I began to learn each investment flow from different investors. From my experience these two different investors are loyal to their field and they rarely cross over to the other. I am here to tell you that it can be extremely profitable invest in both.

Real estate is the most popular and reliable long-term vehicle that an investor can venture into. For years people have taken their investment funds and placed them into the housing market to go on and earn thousands and sometimes millions of dollars. There will always be some daunting measures in real estate due to the fluctuation of housing value and economy. What makes real estate investing so reliable is that it's a constant that'll forever be needed by the public. So the business will forever be profitable, if exercised properly.

To be successful in real estate you must take the time to study and put forth effort to learn the concepts. It's not as difficult as it seems if you have the will power and ambition. To begin you must read a few books to gain the concept, but I'll discuss some of the basics now. Let's begin with the old saying that it takes money to make money.

The first step is to secure an initial investment and you can accomplish this if you followed the previous financial steps. In order to raise the money through banks and/or other forms you will need to have A-1 credit. With a great credit score you will be able to apply and be approved for a loan on a house easily. With this method you'll be able to gain the initial investment without putting much or any of you own money down. So, treat this meeting, as you would any meeting: presentable, professional and with a printed and dressed plan.

If your credit still isn't good enough to get the full loan for the initial investment, there are other options. Once you've found a nice house with potential to produce a profit then you must go through an assessment process to assess the value of the house. You do this by talking with the seller then scheduling a time to visit the place. You then have a title officer check the property and bring a good property accessor with you to view.

In order to find the right price, you have to buy the house with enough equity and value in it. Equity is pure ownership. Once you determine the true value of the home as is you must discover the market value. Market value is simply the price that the house will potentially sell for on the current market once renovated or the ARV. You evaluate both prices but only agree to a price that allows you to make a decent profit.

After you've agreed on a purchase price its time to take this house to the bank. You will write up a decent proposal with all the important financial informatio, cost to profit ratio and meet with an officer at the bank. What you are attempting to gain is an H.E.L.O.C. or home equity line of credit. This is a strategy where the bank buys the house at a percentage of the after-renovation value in exchange for a percentage of equity of the property. You will in turn either fix the property up to sell it in a flip and pay back the loan to pocket the profit. Or the other option will be to renovate and rent the house out in order to pay a monthly mortgage bill to the bank and pocket a small profit each month.

There are plenty of strategies that if executed correctly can generate a hefty profit. The number 1 rule to this venture is to buy the house at a low price to renovate in order to sell high. There are different ways to find these housing investments. To truly learn the ins and outs of real estate will take a great amount of study in more in-depth books.

Investing in other businesses- Another form of investment vehicle consists of the process of investing in up-and-coming businesses. It's sort of like taking on the role of a hard money lender and it comes with its perks. The goal here is to either find or advertise to have a business find you in order to invest in it to yield profit. Not just any business, this business has to have the potential to be successful. So the plan is to do your own due diligence.

To evaluate the business you will require a business plan or a proposal portfolio. This portfolio will give you a glimpse inside of the business and their financial capabilities. You will meet with the owner and/or representative in order establish the reason and means for your investment. If the business is already up and running, take the time to visit some of the business sites to get an idea of how it runs.

If everything checks out, you will set conditions for the use and repayment of your money through a legally binding contractual agreement. These conditions can vary. Due to the nature of your investment, you can require a higher interest rate than a normal loan. A part of your conditions can include a percentage of equity in the company in which you will become part owner. You may also require a position in the administration in order to oversee your investment. The choice is yours to present but each side will have to agree.

Another form of business investment is through the franchising vehicle. This is a process that has been used by many investors on their way to gaining wealth. There are many franchises that you can invest in such as restaurants, stores, gyms, etc. Once you've chosen your category and the particular business that you want to franchise, you will contact the franchise's business office to inquire about joining.

The franchise representative will set up a meeting with you in order to start a business relationship. This will be sort of on interview between you and the business. You will fill out an application that will be used to verify your financial ability to be a franchise owner. In contrast you will interview with the rep with questions regarding the franchise's profit yield margins and their ability to provide. This will be the gist of the first meeting.

If the first meet goes we'll and both sides are satisfied then a second meeting will be scheduled. This meeting will be a bit more entertaining because by now your ability to provide funding should be certified. The franchise rep will provide you with a full tour of some of their main operations. This will include a good stay, great food, and the works because this is the sale pitch to win you over.

Once y decide if this is the franchise you want you will be required to pay the upfront franchise fee. This fee will be a rather lump sum, but you don't have to pay it all initially. If you've been successful in building. A-I credit you can use it to apply for a loan to purchase. You will also be required to pay monthly or quarterly franchise fees that will be paid from your business profit. This is okay because the franchise will provide some amenities.

The franchise will provide you with the quality of its own business model. The two of you will work together to find the best area for your brick and mortar. The franchise will aid you in building the store and providing the materials needed to run the store. The franchise will send an experienced executive to your store to help get you started and to aid in hiring and training your new staff. You will also gain the strong advertising machine behind the franchise. These are some of the nice perks if you are ambitious enough to work it. If this isn't your cup of tea, I have another option if you are willing to bet your life on it.

Life insurance

Life insurance is an multi-faceted vehicle that offers many different features. Many people know of its main purposes which are to support you with heath costs, burial costs and to help provide for your family after death. Most people aren't knowledgeable of life insurance's other features such as; funding and investing. That's right, your life insurance can do much more than get you cheaper hospital bills and buy you a casket.

When you apply for and are approved for a life insurance policy you are making an investment that is backed up by your life. Your policy gives you a rather lump sum of insurance benefits that are subject to be paid under certain conditions. The cash amount of these benefits is to be determined by your insurance company by assessing your health, life and your financial capabilities. This sum is then used to help pay for hospital payments and bills for your burial ceremony and leave the remainder of the policy to your beneficiaries. All of this for an initial deposit and a predetermined monthly premium. That's not all.

Did you know that your insurance policy can act as a loan for important personal acquisitions and business funding? If you indeed apply for a whole life insurance policy, you then borrow against that lump sum in order to fund a business venture. You then in turn will be able to make payments towards this policy through your premium as long as the policy is active. If you are to breach this contract then your policy is void and all money is due.

So life insurance is truly a money investment that uses your life as collateral. This form of funding is rarely known but it can be very valuable. Some of the wealthiest people have used this type of life insurance to gain success. The problem is that some people will abuse this vehicle and lose their rights for quality life insurance. So be warned that when preparing to use this method to please be careful and make good decisions.

Section 5:

Giving Back- Introduction

This will be final section but it's a topic that is close to my heart. Throughout your path to success, you will encounter different classes of people – some are well off, some are not so well off, but some are barely making it by. It's true that some are succumbed to this hardship due to the lack of ambition and motivation.Remember, that there are lot of people on this level who are living without due to their environment, lack of resources and knowledge. All of these people deserve charity in one form of another. I know because I come from a neighborhood of hardship.

Where Im from there isn't a heavy supply of resources and as I've previously noted there is a lack of qualified role models. Jobs are hard to come by and the schools lack the proper tools to fully educate. So the only success we see is from that of crime. This causes unavoidable recidivism and a high rate of incarceration. The lack of knowledge and will, inspires a generation of people dependent on the government.

I know that for some there is no other option forsurvival but there are a lot of people that have the ability and God given talents to be successful and independent. It's our duty to society and to the future of generations to come to help aid our people. Some people live their whole lives without experiencing a better way of life and there is a much better way to live. It is great to help them financially but even better to help them mentally and emotionally. If you teach a child to fish, you have taught him a skill to feed themselves for life.

So instead of just giving money let's give back to our environment. We do this by sharing our knowledge with the people seeking. We do this by setting up ways for these people to gain much needed resources. This should mean more to us than a tax break at the end of the year. This should be our way of life. So, let's discuss some of the ways that you can give back.

Volunteering

We all can benefit from donating some of our spare time for the better good of humanity. There are countless organizations in our communities that are short staffed and need faithful volunteers. It's as easy as finding a cause that you are passionate about and vounteering. Once you apply, you can volunteer at a time that will fit in your schedule. There are various causes to choose from.

There are countless organizations that tend to the homeless if that's a cause that you're interested in. Most of the organizations have kitchens in the heart of the community that feed the homeless throughout the week. These kitchens are always looking for people to help serve food. You could always take your time to make care packages for the homeless. These care packages can contain all sorts of items that they may need such as hygiene products, socks, clothing, a few dollars, etc. Then you take them and pass them all out in areas where the disadvantaged frequently visit.

Working with the youth in the community can be very rewarding. This will help in molding the future generations. You could help in multiple ways at these organizations such as volunteer at your local boys and girls club to teaching a fitness class. If you have a trade, you could help teach a class to help teenagers learn knowledge of the trade. You could possibly, just pick some parks and clean them up in your spare time. Anything is plenty my friend. If you are looking to be more involved than there is another option.

Non – Profit

If you have a vision and passion that you want to give to the world then it's time to share. You could start your own nonprofit organization. The non-profits are very easy and inexpensive to start. All you have to do is put together a plan that displays your purpose. This plan should outline every benefit that you will offer. Once you created this detailed plan, it's time to file for your nonprofit.

Legalizing your nonprofit is easy and you can do it online. You will pay a one-time fee and viola. You will need to have a board of directors. This board of directors should be a mix of professional people that can contribute to the organization. It would help to put a local business owner on the board as this could help with funding.

In order to establish funding you will have to first establish a cause and effect. You should be able to explain this cause and give a reason of why it is deserving of donations. For example, starting an after school organization will give kids something to do after school; this will in turn will have less kids idle; less crime and this will attract more production to this community. Whatever you decide to do be sure to make it count because time is money, and we must manipulate the clock!

Resources

Sample Business Plan Outline:

Table of Contents

I. Executive Summary

A. Brief Overview

B. Total Project Costs

II. Market Analysis

A. Industry Trends

B. Total Market

C. Target Market

    D. Competition

    E. Suppliers

    III. Marketing Plan

    A. Overall Strategy

    B. Products/Services

    C. Pricing

    D. Place

    E. Promotion

    IV. Management Plan

    A. Organizational Structure

    B. Staffing Plan

    C. Job Descriptions

    D. Resumes

    E. Key Operational Functions

    F. Optional Plans & Policies

    V. Financial Data

    A. Personal Financial Statement

    B. Historical Data (if existing business)

    C. Projection Assumptions

    D. P&L and Cash Flow Projections

    E. Projected Balance Sheet

    F. Amortization Schedule

Resources for recently released inmates:

Companies That Hire Felons List

Credit to: HelpForFelons.org

AAMCO Transmissions
Abbott Laboratories
Ace Hardware
Alamo Rent a Car
Alaska Airlines
Alberto-Culver
Allstate Insurance
Allstate Insurance
America West Air
American Airlines
American Express
American Greetings
Anderson Windows
AON Computer
Archer Daniel's Midland
ARCO
Arthur J. Gallagher & Co
AT&T
Atlas Van Lines
Avis Rent-A-Car
Avon Products
Baskin-Robbins
Baxter International
Best Foods
Best Western

BF Goodrich

Black and Decker

Blue Cross/Blue Shield

Boeing

Bridgestone/Firestone

British Airways

Budget Rent-A-Car

Calvin Klein

Campbell Soups

Canon USA

Career Education Group

Carrier

Casio, Inc.

Caterpillar

Chase Bank

Chicago Mercantile Exchange

Cintas

Circuit City

Coldwell Banker

Compaq Computer

ConAgra Foods

Dairy Queen

DAP Products

Deer & Co

Del Monte Foods

Dell Corporation

Delta Air Lines

Delta Faucets

Denny's Inc.

Dollar Rent a Car

Dole Foods

Domino's Pizza

Dow Brands

Dunkin Donuts

Dunlop Tires

DuPont Co.

Duracell

Eddie Bauer

Epson

Equity Office Property

Exelon

Exxon

Federal Express

First Health Group

Fortune Brands

Fruit of the Loom

Fuji

General Electric

General Growth Properties

General Mills

GMAC

Hanes Hosiery

Hewitt associates

Hilton Hotels

- IBM
- Illinois Tool Works
- Kraft Foods
- K-Mart
- L.A. Times
- McDonalds
- Mobil Oil
- Molex
- Navistar International
- Motorola
- New York Times
- Newsweek
- Niki
- NiSource
- Northern Trust
- Old Republic
- Packaging Corp of America
- PACTIV
- PepsiCo
- Phillip Morris
- R.R Donnelley
- Rubbermaid Inc.
- Sara-Lee
- Sears & Roebuck
- ServiceMaster
- Seven Up, Inc.
- Shell Oil

Showtime Networks

Smurfit-Stone Container Corp.

Sony

Southwest Air

Sprint

Target

Telephone & Data Systems

Tellabs

Toys R Us

Tribune Co

U.S Cellular

Uneven Investments

United Airlines

Verizon

W.W Grainger

Walgreens

Wal-Mart

Wrigley Co

Zebra Technologies Group

Zenith Electronics

Xerox

AirTran

Albertson's

American Greetings

American National Logistics

Applebee's

Aramark Food Services
Bahama Breeze
Bally's Hotel & Casino
Bed, Bath & Beyond
Borgata Casino & Spa
Braum's Inc.
Brunswick Corp
Buffalo Wild Wings
Candlewood Suites
Cambell's Soup
Carl's Jr.
Chipotle
Chrysler
Comcast
Comfort Inn &Suites
Darden Restaurants
Dart Containers
Deer Park Spring Water co.
Divizio Industries
Dollar Tree
Dr Pepper/Seven Up
Electrolux
Embassy Suites
Equity Office Properties
ERMCO, Inc.
Fairfield Inn
Florilli Transportation, LLC

Flying J

Food Services of America

Galuoub Toys

Genentech

Golden Corral

Goodwill

Great Clips

Hampton Inn

Hawthorn Suites

HH Gregg

Hilton Hotels

Holiday Inn

Home Depot

Ikea

Jack in the Box

Jiffy Lube

Jimmy Johns

Kelly Moore Paints

KFC

Kohl's

Labor Ready

Lowes

Luby's

Maggiano's

Marriott Hotels

Men's Wearhouse

Metals USA

Miller Brewing Company

Coors Brewing Company

Rubbermaid

Nordstrom

O'Charleys

OIX, Inc.

Old Republic International

Olive Garden

Omni Direct

Pappadeaux

Party City

Perkins Restaurants

PetSmart

Radisson

Red Lobster

Red Robin

Residence Inn

Restaurant Depot

Reyes Beverage Group

Ross

RSC Equipment Rental

Revel Hotel Resort & Casino

Safeway

Salvation Army

Sara Lee

Seasons 52

Sharaton Hotels

Shoprite

Simplex Leasing

Sisbro, Inc.

Springhill Suites

Starwood Hotels

Subway

Sysco

Teleperformance

TGI Friday

Towneplace Suites

Trader Joes

Tradewinds

Tribune Company

Tyson Foods

U-Haul

Grants for recently released inmates:

Department of Labor Grants

The Department of Labor; Employment and Training Administration has several grant programs for felons that are pre-release as well as for ex-felons that are out of prison. Most grants are also open to anyone who applies whether they are a felon or not.

These loans cover many different things from housing, transportation, small businesses and community development. You can search or browse all available grants here on Grants.Gov. Simply go to their website, search and then fill out the application package associated with each grant opportunity.

Educational Pell Grants for Felons

Pell Grants are only available for educational purposes and are open to almost all felons. Drug related felonies will bar you from receiving a Pell Grant, but this can be overcome if you have or complete an approved drug rehabilitation program and also pass two random drug tests.

Students or aspiring students with criminal convictions have limited eligibility for federal student aid but nearly 100% of cases can be overcome in one way or another. Here is where you can find information on Pell Grants or apply directly.

Pell Grants are available to use at any approved and credentialed college or trade school. Since white collar jobs often discriminate against felons it may be worth investigating blue collar trade schools. Many trade schools offer programs in welding, carpentry, electrical, roofing, drafting/CAD and HVAC (Heating Ventilation Air Conditioning). Often times we have found that construction and trade type jobs are much more apt to hire a felon than other white collar or office type jobs.

Acknowledgements

First, I want to thank the staff and administration at Hinds Community College for providing a great establishment for our society to gain knowledge and further their education. I want to thank Mr. Brooks for being a great mentor and instructor for all the students at Hind , including myself.

I dedicate this book to my family, whether family through bloodline or family through life such as my niece Latrice, my brothers Willie Earl and Jeffrey, my uncles that taught me a trade, my beautiful daughters and handsome son., my best friend Marcus and my friend and business partner Marlon. Most of all I dedicate this book to my mother Corine Hill, my sister Cheryl Bennett, my grandmother Helen Hill and my father Jesse Anderson; may you all rest in heaven.

www.ingramcontent.com/pod-product-compliance
Lightning Source LLC
Chambersburg PA
CBHW071521220526
45472CB00003B/1104